Crime Scene Investigation

Crime Scene Investigation

Barbara Harris
Kris Kohlmeier
Robert D. Kiel

Teacher Ideas Press
An Imprint of Greenwood Publishing Group
361 Hanover Street
Portsmouth, New Hampshire
1999

This book is dedicated to all past, present, and future Windsor Castle Students

TEACHER IDEAS PRESS
An Imprint of Greenwood Publishing Group
361 Hanover Street
Portsmouth, NH 03801
1-800-225-5800
www.teacherideaspress.com

Production Editors: Stephen Haenel and Felicity Tucker
Copy Editor: Melissa R. Root
Proofreader: Eileen Bartlett
Indexer: Linda Running Bentley
Typesetter: Michael Florman

Library of Congress Cataloging-in-Publication Data

Harris, Barbara, 1948-
  Crime scene investigation / Barbara Harris, Kris Kohlmeier,
Robert D. Kiel.
    xiii, 109 p. 22x28 cm.
    Includes index.
    ISBN 1-56308-637-9 (softbound)
    1. Crime scene searches--Study and teaching--Activity programs.
  2. Middle school education--Activity programs. I. Kohlmeier, Kris.
  II. Kiel, Robert D. III. Title.
    HV8073 .H28 1999
    363.25--dc21
                                                      98-51476
                                                         CIP

Contents

Foreword

Henry Adams has been quoted as saying, "A teacher affects eternity; he can never tell where his influence stops." The outcomes for students who participate in the Crime Scene Investigation Project are a true testament to this thought. The influence of this learning opportunity will result in future lawyers, police officers, journalists, judges—the list of possibilities goes on, for the middle school students in Windsor Castle as well as for all middle school students afforded this opportunity.

In recent years, Woodrow Wilson Middle School took on the challenges found in the National Task Force study "Caught in the Middle." Teachers were faced with the dilemma of planning interdisciplinary units of study to be used as tools for multidisciplinary team teaching. This book was created and designed by a group of teachers who had a vision about the importance of thematic teaching for their students. Within these pages, you will find a nationally recognized interdisciplinary unit filled with proven strategies, worksheets, and encouraging ideas to help students learn and succeed. Given few tools, Barbara Harris, Bob Kiel, and Kris Kohlmeier sat down to work together to achieve the goal of thematic learning for their team of students. The Crime Scene Investigation is an exciting unit that lends itself to integrated learning opportunities taught through English, history, and science classes. Throughout the project, students become active participants in the learning process while working in cooperative groups. Gifted students are challenged through critical thinking situations, and exciting hands-on opportunities are accessible to second language learners.

I have seen the influence that this interdisciplinary unit has had on middle school students. They thirst for knowledge and are eager as they anticipate the outcomes that are being discovered. This book represents hours of work by the team teachers of Windsor Castle who are known for their ability to care about kids while making learning meaningful and fun. I know that this unit will be a valuable resource to all middle school teachers in their quest for quality education for their students.

Cheryl McCartney
Assistant Principal

Acknowledgments

Thanks to our families and friends for their
continued support and encouragement in the
Crime Scene Investigation.

Preface

Crime Scene Investigation is the result of the authors' work together as an interdisciplinary team. Five years ago, our school changed from a junior high to a middle school. Keeping in mind middle school philosophy and practices, we wanted to develop an interdisciplinary unit that would be innovative, exciting, and fun for our students.

As we have grown as a team, the unit we created, Crime Scene Investigation, has grown as a project. Each year we have added more facets to it, changing and adapting to meet our students' needs.

In 1996, we submitted the Crime Scene Investigation unit to Prentice-Hall and the National Middle School Association (NMSA) Teaching Team Awards for consideration for their interdisciplinary unit award. Much to our delight, we were chosen as one of the four national grand prize winners for the western region of the United States. We were guests of Prentice-Hall and the National Middle School Association at the NMSA conference in Baltimore, Maryland, in October, 1996. We presented our winning project at a focus session.

Since then, we have conducted in-service workshops on teaming and creating inter-disciplinary units. We have used the Crime Scene Investigation as an interdisciplinary unit to maximize student learning in a team setting.

This project can be used by both experienced and inexperienced teams. We hope you and your students enjoy the Crime Scene Investigation activity. We encourage you to use this book as a model to develop your own interdisciplinary unit.

Introduction

Interdisciplinary units are more than just the latest fad in education. They are great ways for teachers to get students actively involved while teaching the core curriculum. These units can stimulate curiosity, make abstract concepts more concrete, and include a variety of learning strategies. The best part—they are just plain fun!

Crime Scene Investigation does all of these things and more. It is a hands-on investigative approach to solving a real-life problem. Students investigate a crime and solve a mystery step-by-step. The unit includes role-playing, skill development in writing, research, and computers. Its focus is skill development in science, English, and history in a team setting. The project includes an interdisciplinary team portfolio, which shows students how each aspect of the curriculum is related and blended together to solve a crime mystery. This is an engaging project for students of all levels of ability—from Limited English Proficient and Special Education to Gifted and Talented.

This Crime Scene Investigation unit is an interdisciplinary activity that brings together teams to solve a common problem. Individual classes can also use the investigation as a class activity. The unit is designed so that it allows you to change and to adapt to your team, school setting, and educational objectives.

As we guide you through this exciting activity, you will see your students challenged to use all their skills and talents from different subject areas to solve a common problem. As you present and guide your students through the Crime Scene Investigation, your students' imaginations and innate interest in puzzles and problem solving will generate tremendous energy and excitement for this student-centered investigation.

As your students become involved in this activity, all students' abilities and skills will be challenged at an appropriate involvement level for them. For all levels of students, suggestions will be provided along the way as to how to adapt and provide for special needs.

The Crime Scene Investigation will be explained and organized for you in terms of how to prepare, present, and conduct this student-centered activity. The unit brings together primarily English, history, and science students to understand and solve a real-life-like problem. As this activity is developed, it will also be explained how to include other subject areas and how to use school and community resources. After you and your students have participated in this investigation, you will be given guidance in developing your own Crime Scene Investigation.

So teachers, have your students become detectives. Grab a notepad, a pencil, and a magnifying glass, and let's begin!

Chapter One

Overview of Crime Scene Investigation

Crime Scene Investigation is an interdisciplinary unit that combines skills in many subject areas. Science, English, and history are the core areas, but art, math, and technology are also involved (figure 1-1). All levels of students can participate successfully.

Fig. 1-1. Interdisciplinary Team Activity

Team Effort

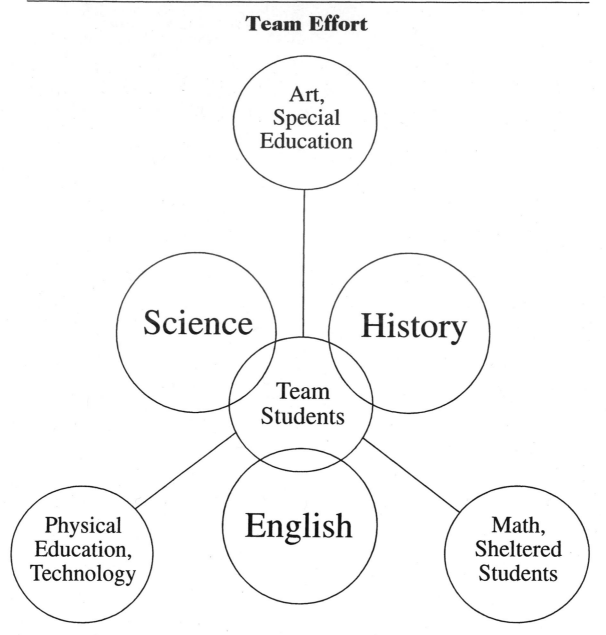

The Crime Scene Investigation integrates curriculum so students can see connections between subject areas (figure 1-2). The project enhances self-esteem, career awareness, and cooperative learning. Students engage in real-life experiences. Both school and community resources are used. Students role-play and use their creativity while still using content area skills.

Fig. 1-2. Integrating the Curriculum

Science-English-History

The project begins with a letter sent home to parents. The excitement builds with each step along the way. Your students will be investigating the crime scene, analyzing evidence, engaging in interviews of witnesses and suspects, writing police reports and news stories, applying for jobs related to the trial, and conducting a mock trial (figure 1-3). At the trial's conclusion, the students will agree this activity was a worthwhile learning experience, and one they will not soon forget!

Fig. 1-3. Planning the Interdisciplinary Activity

Active, Involved, Student-Oriented Team Project

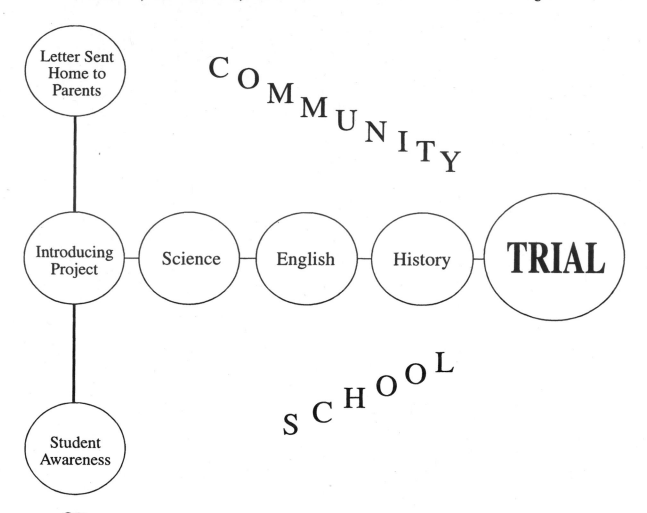

THE CRIME

The setting for this Crime Scene Investigation is the school library. Several students have set up a display of their personal collections of sports cards and antique dolls. The student display is to remain in the library for several days. Some of the pieces in the collection are displayed in small glass display cases and some on library tables. The student collection is said to be valued at about $2,500.

As the students set up the display during the afternoon, other students and teachers stop by to help set up and to ask questions. As the school day comes to an end, students and teachers leave the library, until it is silent and empty.

Suddenly, a loud crashing noise penetrates the hallway. A teacher comes out into the hallway to investigate. Looking up and down the hall to determine where the sound has come from, the teacher sees three suspicious-looking individuals running out of the library, each carrying a large brown bag. It appears to the teacher that they are two boys and a girl wearing dark clothing. The teacher does not know the students by name.

The teacher calls out to the three students to stop. The students turn and look in the direction of the teacher, and then run and exit the building. The teacher does not think about the incident much more and leaves for home about an hour after school is out.

The next day as the custodian opens the building, he notices that the student display has been tampered with, and materials are scattered. It appears that parts of the display are missing. The custodian calls for the police, who soon arrive to take witness statements and collect physical evidence.

You will be guided in organizing and setting up the following:

- The teacher and student witnesses who saw the student display being set up in the library.

- The students who will testify to what was in their collections and what the value was.

- The teacher witness who saw suspects leaving the library in a hurry after the crashing sound.

- The setup of the crime scene in the library so that physical evidence may be collected.

- The interviewing of witnesses and the collection of physical evidence.

- The analyzing and comparing of physical evidence with suspects, and the writing of reports.

- The filling out of police reports, and the writing of newspaper articles.

- Preparing for the trial.

- Conducting the trial.

- Creating a notebook/portfolio of the Crime Scene Investigation.

Working together as an interdisciplinary team, the students are guided step-by-step to role-play, to collect and evaluate evidence, to write newspaper and police reports, and to conduct a trial to bring the case to a conclusion.

 THE INVESTIGATORS

Science

Science students become actively involved in the Crime Scene Investigation. They are called upon to go to the crime scene to investigate and collect physical evidence (figure 1-4).

In investigative teams composed of police officers and lab technicians, students will use proper procedures and skills they have learned to collect, bag, and label the physical evidence they discover at the library crime scene. As the investigative teams work their way through the crime scene, the students will collect discovered pieces of physical evidence, such as fingerprints, shoe prints, hair, handwritten notes, and cloth fibers. For accuracy and for better understanding of the crime scene, investigative team members will draw a map of the library and indicate where physical evidence is discovered and collected.

As students return to science class, the classroom is transformed into an investigative crime lab. Here in the lab, students take several days to analyze and describe the physical evidence found in the library. Once the evidence has been evaluated, it is compared to evidence taken from the suspects.

You will be providing the students with evidence taken from the three suspects. As investigative teams take custody of this evidence, they will try to determine if there is a match between evidence taken from the crime scene and evidence taken from the three suspects.

Science students will bring this part of the activity to a conclusion as they determine if there is enough physical evidence to bring the suspects to trial. In a final evaluation of physical evidence, students will determine that there are several matches between evidence from the crime scene and evidence from the suspects. This evidence combined with witness interviews will strongly suggest to the students that the suspects need to be brought to trial to determine their guilt or innocence.

Science team students will again be called upon for their skills in the trial as criminologists testifying in court that the evidence found at the crime scene does or does not match evidence taken from the suspects.

Your students will test and apply their science skills in this investigation. They will have individual evidence of their skills and the information they have learned as they start assembling their Crime Scene Investigation portfolio.

English

Listening, Speaking, Reading, Writing

The English section of the project emphasizes listening, speaking, reading, and writing (figure 1-5). Working as investigative teams, the students think and work as detectives and news reporters. Students begin by interviewing witnesses to the crime. They prepare questions in advance to ask the witnesses when they question them in the library. Working with a partner, they compare answers from each witness, gather the facts, and prepare to write a news story.

Here is an opportunity to bring in community resources. Arrange for a reporter from the local paper to come into the classroom to talk to the students about how he or she covers a story.

Fig. 1-4. The Crime Scene
(Science)

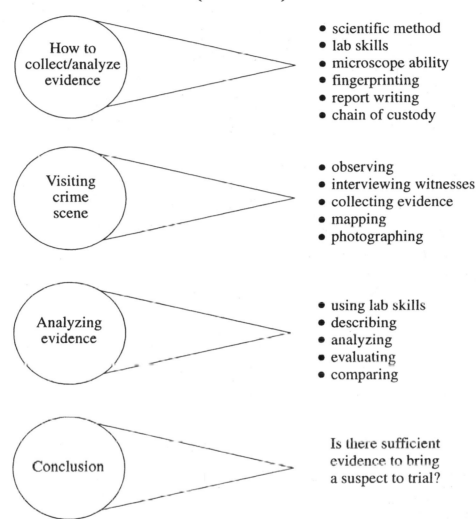

How to collect/analyze evidence
- scientific method
- lab skills
- microscope ability
- fingerprinting
- report writing
- chain of custody

Visiting crime scene
- observing
- interviewing witnesses
- collecting evidence
- mapping
- photographing

Analyzing evidence
- using lab skills
- describing
- analyzing
- evaluating
- comparing

Conclusion

Is there sufficient evidence to bring a suspect to trial?

Students will analyze an article they have brought in from a newspaper before they write their own. They will see what elements to include (who, what, when, where, why, and how). They will then write their own Crime Scene Investigation news article using facts about the crime and quotations from witnesses. After peers have edited the news articles, the final copy is typed on the computer.

Another opportunity to use community resources would involve inviting a police officer to discuss criminal investigations and to instruct the students on how to fill out police and evidence reports. Students then learn to pay close attention to detail, and they see that writing is an important skill in most jobs.

Fig. 1-5. Police Report—News Media

(English)

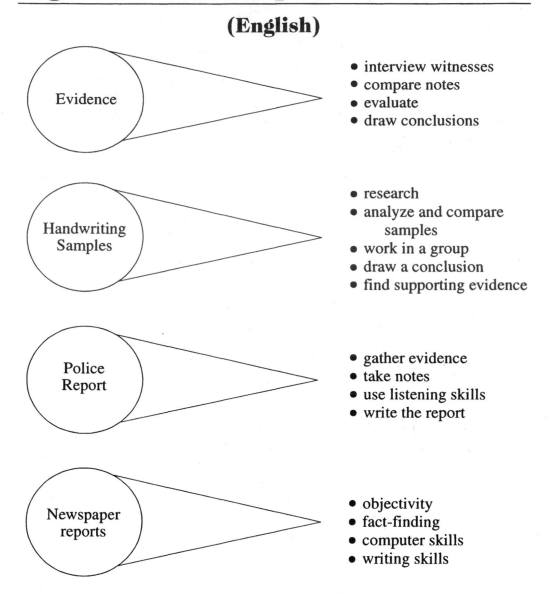

Evidence
- interview witnesses
- compare notes
- evaluate
- draw conclusions

Handwriting Samples
- research
- analyze and compare samples
- work in a group
- draw a conclusion
- find supporting evidence

Police Report
- gather evidence
- take notes
- use listening skills
- write the report

Newspaper reports
- objectivity
- fact-finding
- computer skills
- writing skills

Using books from the school library on handwriting analysis, students analyze a note left behind at the crime scene. Working with a partner first, the student's own handwriting is analyzed. The partners then try to match a suspect's handwriting to the note left behind at the scene of the crime. Paying close attention to detail, the students write a paragraph supporting their conclusion.

The mystery genre is the literary component. Students read mystery stories or a novel and write a scene or a story of their own. They can base this story on the crime scene, or they can use another example.

An interdisciplinary team portfolio concludes the project. Students evaluate each part. They tell what they liked, what they didn't like, and what they learned. They can offer suggestions for improvement.

Your students will have the experience of becoming detectives, reporters, journalists, authors, and critics in a realistic setting created by the Crime Scene Investigation.

History/Social Science

In social studies, the students use their skills of researching, reasoning, higher-level critical thinking, and cooperative learning to work their way through this interdisciplinary team activity.

In preparation for the project, students will have spent approximately two months studying the United States Constitution, the Bill of Rights, and the other amendments (figure 1-6). With this project, the students have the opportunity to put their knowledge of the Constitution, the law, police procedures, and courtroom procedures to work.

Students will have the opportunity to apply for jobs pertaining to the trial, such as attorneys, suspects, criminologists, courtroom personnel, and television and print news reporters. Students will fill out job applications as if they were applying for real jobs. Students will be assigned to their jobs based on their interests and personal strengths.

Once students are assigned jobs, they will research their tasks and prepare for their roles. Instruction will be given to guide them through their tasks and the trial. Student excitement will build as the trial nears!

THEN THE TRIAL BEGINS!

As we guide you through the procedure, students develop their own questions, answers, and line of defense. The project culminates as the verdicts are read.

The students have followed this case from the beginning to the end to determine the guilt or innocence of the suspects. They have integrated the skills of science, English, and history as they relate to the real world.

Tapping into the Resources of the School and Community

This interdisciplinary team activity primarily involves science, English, and history. However, there are many opportunities to involve other subject areas and school and community resources. As you bring these resources into your Crime Scene Investigation, this student-involved activity becomes more of a schoolwide community project.

During the trial, you may want to invite art classes to come in and sketch the trial and its participants. Other classes can be involved by becoming members of the jury. Because the trial will be held in the school auditorium, you may wish to invite other classes to attend as an audience. Math classes may be involved to make timelines, charts, graphs, and various calculations.

Fig. 1-6. Constitutional Rights

The Trial (History)

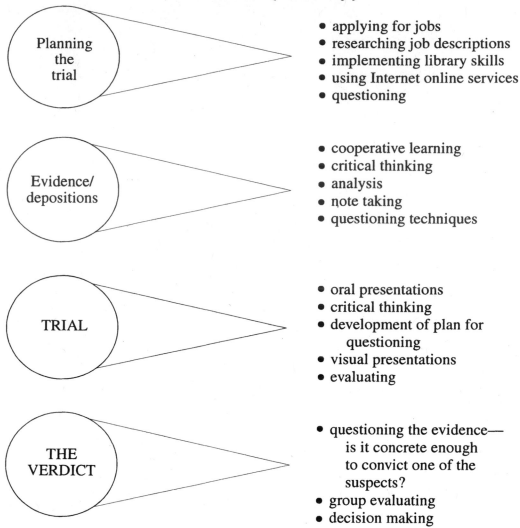

Planning the trial
- applying for jobs
- researching job descriptions
- implementing library skills
- using Internet online services
- questioning

Evidence/depositions
- cooperative learning
- critical thinking
- analysis
- note taking
- questioning techniques

TRIAL
- oral presentations
- critical thinking
- development of plan for questioning
- visual presentations
- evaluating

THE VERDICT
- questioning the evidence— is it concrete enough to convict one of the suspects?
- group evaluating
- decision making

Experts from the community can be invited into your classrooms to help link this activity to the real world and to job skills. Police officers can explain how to collect and analyze the physical evidence. Newspaper writers can explain how to conduct interviews. Attorneys and judges can explain people's legal rights and how a trial is conducted. Legal experts can also act as judges during the trial.

As we develop the Crime Scene Investigation, opportunities to bring in experts will be explained. When you bring in school and community resources, you will have a more exciting and educationally rewarding investigation. We will also explain how you can develop you own investigation.

From *Crime Scene Investigation.* © 1999 Barbara Harris, Kris Kohlmeier, and Robert D. Kiel. Teacher Ideas Press. (800)237-6124

Chapter Two

Timeline

In this section, you will get an idea of how much time you will need to run the Crime Scene Investigation with your students (figure 2-1). Alter the time formats as needed to fit your program and curriculum. The Crime Scene Investigation takes six weeks. One thing is certain: You will need two to three days to conduct the trial!

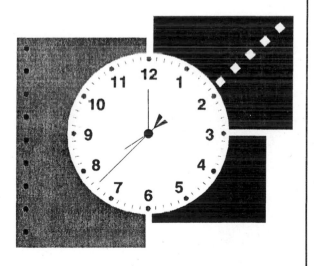

Fig. 2-1. Timeline Overview

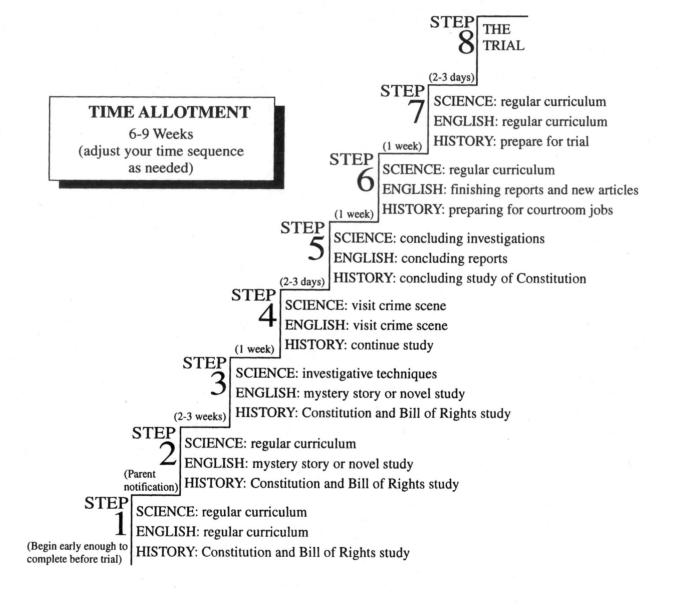

TIME ALLOTMENT
6-9 Weeks
(adjust your time sequence
as needed)

STEP 8 THE TRIAL

(2-3 days)

STEP 7
SCIENCE: regular curriculum
ENGLISH: regular curriculum
HISTORY: prepare for trial

(1 week)

STEP 6
SCIENCE: regular curriculum
ENGLISH: finishing reports and new articles
HISTORY: preparing for courtroom jobs

(1 week)

STEP 5
SCIENCE: concluding investigations
ENGLISH: concluding reports
HISTORY: concluding study of Constitution

(2-3 days)

STEP 4
SCIENCE: visit crime scene
ENGLISH: visit crime scene
HISTORY: continue study

(1 week)

STEP 3
SCIENCE: investigative techniques
ENGLISH: mystery story or novel study
HISTORY: Constitution and Bill of Rights study

(2-3 weeks)

STEP 2
SCIENCE: regular curriculum
ENGLISH: mystery story or novel study
HISTORY: Constitution and Bill of Rights study

(Parent notification)

STEP 1
SCIENCE: regular curriculum
ENGLISH: regular curriculum
HISTORY: Constitution and Bill of Rights study

(Begin early enough to complete before trial)

From *Crime Scene Investigation*. © 1999 Barbara Harris, Kris Kohlmeier, and Robert D. Kiel. Teacher Ideas Press. (800)237-6124

13

 STEP ONE:
CRIME SCENE INVESTIGATION STARTUP

Time: Start early enough to finish before trial date.

- Begin a study of the United States Constitution, Bill of Rights, and the remaining amendments to the Constitution. (Allow approximately $1\frac{1}{2}$ to 2 months).

- Focus on the powers of the government and the responsibilities of each branch of government. Also focus on individual rights as provided for in the Bill of Rights.

- Consult the many sources that offer studies of the Constitution and the Bill of Rights. Such materials can be of great value and can help guide you and your students through your study. However, the *best* curriculum available is the kind that you make up for your students.

CURRICULUM AREAS

Science: Study regular curriculum.
English: Study regular curriculum.
History: Begin the study of the Constitution, Bill of Rights, and remaining amendments.

 STEP TWO:
COMMUNICATION HOME

Time: One month before Step Three.

Send a letter home to parents informing them of this upcoming team project. Explain that students will be investigating an imaginary crime that has taken place at school. Each student will be investigating the crime by visiting the crime scene, taking fingerprints, collecting hair and cloth evidence, comparing shoe prints, and analyzing handwriting left at the scene. The letter can also explain that students will be interviewing witnesses and suspects, filling out police reports, and filling out evidence reports. As students learn how our legal system works through this investigation, they will have the opportunity to role-play police officers, attorneys, and newspaper writers. Explain in the letter that the culminating event will be the trial to determine the guilt or innocence of the suspects. Students will be filling out job applications for courtroom jobs and will begin working in groups to make their case in the court of law. This letter can also be used as an opportunity to ask parents to volunteer their skills, knowledge, and time as it applies to the Crime Scene Investigation.

CURRICULUM AREAS

Science: Study regular curriculum.
English: Begin mystery story or novel study.
History: Continue study of the Constitution, Bill of Rights, and remaining amendments.

STEP THREE:
PREPARATION ACTIVITIES FOR THE CRIME SCENE INVESTIGATION

Time: Two to three weeks.

At this point, the study of the Constitution is well underway, and parents were informed of the project a month earlier by letter. This stage is when the science classes will begin their investigative studies.

Science classes begin study of investigative techniques. Students will learn how to investigate and collect evidence during this stage. This is when you bring in police officers and lab technicians to show students proper techniques of investigation. After students have learned and practiced these techniques, set up the minicrime scene in class, and let them practice their new skills.

History teachers should be stressing constitutional rights during this investigative process so that everyone's right to due process is not violated. This could become an issue during the trial.

CURRICULUM AREAS

Science: Begin investigative techniques and skills study.
English: Continue mystery stories study and regular curriculum.
History: Continue study of the Constitution, Bill of Rights, and remaining amendments.

STEP FOUR:
VISITING THE CRIME SCENE

Time: One week.

At this stage, English and science students will visit the crime scene and will apply their newly practiced skills. English students, working as news reporters and detectives, will first view the crime scene in the library. After viewing the crime scene, students will begin interviewing the witnesses and filling out reports. After the English classes visit the crime scene, the science classes will visit the crime scene to collect physical evidence for evaluation. There will be crossover between science investigative lessons and the English writing and report activities during this stage.

Take one class at a time for the interviews, which should be held like news conferences. If you have five or six classes, you will have five or six interview sessions. Students should have questions ready beforehand.

Next, invite a police officer to class to guide students on how to fill out police reports and evidence reports of the crime. In addition, provide a book on handwriting analysis for the class and begin to teach students about the topic. Students will then write a news article from the point of view of an unbiased news reporter. They should just report the facts of the case.

Finally, science classes will visit the crime scene to collect, bag, and label the physical evidence for analyzing and comparison to suspect evidence.

CURRICULUM AREAS

Science: Continue investigation skills. Students will visit the crime scene the day after the English classes view it, to gather and collect physical evidence.

English: Visit crime scene and interview witnesses. Once witness information is collected, students will work on police reports, prepare evidence reports, write news stories, and analyze handwriting.

History: Continue study of the Constitution, Bill of Rights, and remaining amendments. Stress constitutional rights during the students' investigative processes.

STEP FIVE:
CRIME SCENE REPORTING

Time: Two to three days.

By careful planning and coordination, science, English, and history classes will be finishing their respective parts so they can then start the process for the trial.

Science classes will conclude investigations as the science classroom now becomes the crime lab. The science teacher should allow for some before- and after-school time for students to review evidence, if needed.

English classes will continue with report writing, mystery story writing, and news writing activities during this stage. All reports and stories will become part of the portfolios.

History classes will be wrapping up the study of the Constitution, the Bill of Rights, and the remaining amendments.

STEP SIX: COURTROOM JOBS

Time: One week.

At this stage, students will apply for and be given courtroom jobs. Students will also begin to prepare for the trial.

History students will apply for their courtroom jobs. Using a job application form (see page 83), students will fill out all information. **Remember:** Trials will be conducted through history classes, so if a student wants to work cooperatively with a friend, he or she needs to think of classmates from history classes.

After the submission of the job application form, students are assigned a courtroom job, by you, based on their interests, abilities, neatness of the application, and the needs of the court. Job applications will become part of the portfolios.

You will need to work with the library at this point. Students will then spend a day or so researching what their job really entails. Written descriptions of their jobs will become part of the portfolios.

Invite a police officer, attorney, or judge to come to your classes to explain courtroom procedures. You then want to have that person give the prosecuting team (attorneys, criminologists, police officers, and witnesses) some strategies for the trial. Ask your expert to also advise the defense team (attorneys, criminologists, defendants) on strategies for the trial.

CURRICULUM AREAS

Science: Regular curriculum. Keep crime lab open for the defense and prosecution teams to analyze the evidence.

English: Turn in all reports, conclusions, and news stories in portfolios.

History: Apply for courtroom jobs. Research job requirements. Begin working in teams to prove or disprove the case.

STEP SEVEN: TRIAL PREPARATION

Time: One week.

At this stage, the preparation for the trial begins.

Prosecution and defense teams will work cooperatively to develop their cases. Bailiffs, court reporters, and court clerks will prepare equipment and materials for the courtroom. Witnesses and suspects will study their roles to perfection. They will meet with their respective defense or prosecution teams to solidify their cases. Conduct a practice courtroom scene in class where both sets of attorneys can question the witnesses and suspects. (Allow two days for this practice.)

CURRICULUM AREAS

Science: Regular curriculum/crime lab remains open.
English: Regular curriculum/continue mystery story.
History: Students develop cases and formulate questions. Courtroom personnel are preparing equipment and materials for the courtroom.

STEP EIGHT: THE TRIAL

Time: Two to three days.

THE TRIAL BEGINS!

History classes will conduct the trials. Each history class will conduct its own trial. (If you have five history classes, you will have five trials.) Hold trials in a large room (e.g., the auditorium). The English and science classes will be the audience.

Set up the room like a courtroom. Make arrangements with a stage manager to use microphones, lights, and so forth.

Have classes from different grade levels act as your jury. The trial will take three days. At the conclusion of the trial, verdicts are read.

CURRICULUM AREAS

Science: View the trial.
English: View the trial.
History: Conduct the trial.

Chapter Three

Science Activities and Preparation Prior to the Crime Scene Investigation

As students study science, they gain skills in questioning, predicting, testing, collecting data, evaluating, and drawing conclusions. Your students will have the opportunity to use these skills in investigating and solving the Crime Scene Investigation.

Here are some suggestions, activities, and checklists to help you provide your students with the necessary skills and knowledge to be successful and enjoy the investigation when you begin.

COOPERATIVE TEAMS

In professional fields related to law enforcement, individuals such as police, attorneys, and lab technicians are often times called upon to work together in teams. Frequently in science we call upon our students to work in cooperative teams to do experiments and to solve problems by conducting investigations. In this way we ask our students to share ideas, respect others, and take on specific tasks. These same skills that are used in science will now be put to use to solve the Crime Scene Investigation.

The more time and guidance you have provided your students in working together in cooperative teams, the greater the experience in approaching the Crime Scene Investigation. Guidance from you will make the investigation a rewarding experience.

SCIENTIFIC METHOD

The scientific method is an organized way to approach and solve an identified problem or question. The scientific method is described in a variety of ways. Use this description of the scientific method to help guide your students in approaching and solving a problem in an orderly manner.

The Scientific Method:

1. Identify a problem.
2. Collect information.
3. Develop a hypothesis.
4. Test the hypothesis by making observations and collecting data.
5. Retest if necessary.
6. Draw a conclusion.

Students will be able to transfer their scientific skills into police science skills. The Crime Scene Investigation will allow your students to challenge their scientific skills and solve a real-life problem.

PATTERNS

During the Crime Scene Investigation, students will be called upon to make many comparisons. As they make these comparisons, they are often looking for and identifying patterns. Shoe print and fingerprint patterns may well determine the guilt or innocence of the suspects.

Before the investigation begins, any guidance you have provided your students in identifying and working with patterns in nature will help them in this project. Weeks prior to the investigation, point out and discuss patterns in nature, such as weather, tides, the moon, and others that your students discover.

ROLE-PLAYING

In science class, you may have asked your students to imagine that they were a scientist, astronaut, chemist, or some other individual related to science. You try at times to give your students a sense of what it would be like to be in a different setting or assigned the responsibility of solving a problem.

Role-playing shows students how skills they are learning apply to real-life professions that use those skills. They can use these skills to break down and solve complex problems. Role-playing also allows students to picture themselves in a certain role or job. They may find this activity rewarding enough to go one step further and start thinking about their own future career goals and the relationship of them to their education.

The Crime Scene Investigation allows you, through science, to guide your students into taking on the roles of police officer, investigator, and lab technician. As they participate in these roles, they will apply their classroom science skills to solve real-life problems.

PREPARATORY ACTIVITIES

Fingerprint Activities

Oftentimes in movies or on the news we see how fingerprints are an important part of solving a crime. When fingerprints are available, they can be used as a positive means of identification.

Fingerprints can become an important and realistic part of your investigation. Practice in lifting, identifying, and comparing fingerprints before the investigation is an important preparation activity. If you are just starting with fingerprinting, keep it simple and have fun with it.

Fingerprint Materials

If you are not familiar with fingerprinting, there are three good sources of materials and information for you.

Your local police/sheriff department may be able to provide you with the necessary materials, information, and demonstrations on lifting fingerprints and using them for identification. Invite a police officer or a lab technician into your classroom to give instruction and demonstrations on the use of fingerprinting. This is an excellent way to get started.

A second choice is to find science suppliers who sell fingerprint kits. These kits can provide you with the necessary materials and directions to get started. Check your science catalogs for the materials you will need.

Finally, do not forget to check your school and public library for fingerprinting books that will provide you with background information, classification of fingerprints, and how-to information. You may want to help your school library build a collection of such books so they are available to your students.

Checklist of Suggested Fingerprint Materials:

This is a suggested list of materials you may need in fingerprint activities:

- ✓ One ink pad for each team
- ✓ Extra bottles of ink
- ✓ Fingerprint dusting powder
- ✓ Fingerprint feather-dusting brush
- ✓ Hand lenses
- ✓ Fingerprint application cards
- ✓ Cleaning materials to clean up after fingerprinting
- ✓ Fingerprint classification charts
- ✓ Lunch-size paper bags
- ✓ Clear plastic tape
- ✓ White paper

Using Fingerprint Materials

Ink pads work well for students taking and making their own fingerprints. Extra ink is needed to keep pads adequately inked to make prints that are clear and dark. It is a good idea to practice taking fingerprints for a few minutes.

Fingerprint dusting powder does tend to get on everything. Have cleaning materials available to wash hands and clean up any excess powder.

Make sure you give safety instructions to students before starting any activity. Be sure the instructions you provide are followed.

Suggested Fingerprint Activities

The following suggested activities will help your students develop fingerprinting understanding and skills. The list goes from the simplest to the more challenging activities. Adjust and change these activities and create your own to adapt to your needs and setting.

Suggested activities:

- Have students print their own right thumbprint. Students observe, diagram, and describe their own print.

- Students compare their thumbprint to another student's thumbprint to observe similarities and differences.

- Teach students the fingerprint identification system.

- Have students print all 10 fingerprints on a fingerprint application card. Obtain a fingerprint application card from your local police department.

- Demonstrate how fingerprints are lifted and used for identification.

- Conduct a mini crime activity to demonstrate how students can put these skills to use.
- Explain the history of fingerprints.
- Invite a police officer or a lab technician to your classroom to demonstrate and explain how fingerprints are used as physical evidence for positive identification.

Hair and Cloth Fiber Analysis

Before the Crime Scene Investigation, give instruction and practice time to students to work with and describe hair and cloth fibers. Instruction could be kept at the simple level of describing the physical characteristics of hair and cloth fibers. However, kits are available from science suppliers that can help you describe, analyze, and classify such materials.

In the interests of time and effort, you may want to integrate such instruction after students have been to the crime scene and collected the physical evidence. As students are about to analyze the crime scene evidence in the lab, provide them with the instruction and guidance to analyze hair and cloth fiber.

Shoe Prints

In the actual Crime Scene Investigation, make sure that a shoe print is left behind at the scene of the crime. Each investigative team member will be given a photocopy of the shoe print.

Shoe print samples will be taken from three suspects who have been taken into custody. Students will have the opportunity to compare the shoe print found in the library with the suspects' prints.

Practicing may not be necessary before the actual investigation. After the students have collected the shoe print at the crime scene, they can develop their own procedures and figure out what to look for in making comparisons.

Do not be surprised if students ask to see the bottom of your shoes or the shoes of other students in class. Students will even go to shoe stores to track down the brand of shoe from the crime scene.

Mapping

We often look to a diagram or a map to help us understand an idea or how to get to a certain place. As students visit the crime scene and try to make sense of what has happened, drawing a map of the physical setting may help them to put time and the sequence of events into a proper perspective. Any practice that students have had in drawing diagrams and maps before the Crime Scene Investigation will help them when they draw an actual map of the crime scene.

Other Evidence

The basic pieces of evidence found at the crime scene and activities you may consider conducting with students before the actual Crime Scene Investigation are discussed earlier in this chapter.

Considering you school setting, materials, and resources available, you may want to think about adding or substituting another type of physical evidence if you adapt or change your individual investigation. If you change or substitute physical evidence, consider any prior preparation activities you may want to conduct before the investigation.

Bring in the Experts

As you start putting together your preparation activities, consider asking police officers, lab technicians, and other experts to come into your classroom and give lectures, provide demonstrations, and lead activities on how to properly collect, describe, and analyze the physical evidence.

This is a great time for the experts to explain how basic skills are put to use in their professions. As an interdisciplinary team activity, it is important to guide the students in seeing how all the subject skills come together to solve a common problem.

Mini Crime Scene Investigation

After having given instructions and provided activities to your students in preparation of the Crime Scene Investigation, you may want to culminate these activities with a mini Crime Scene Investigation in your classroom. The guest experts can help you run or create this mini investigation.

This activity will help your students put their skills together and will get them excited about the upcoming investigation. It will allow for some practice and refining of skills before the actual activity takes place. Before class starts, set up several numbered stations in the classroom. At each numbered station, place some piece of physical evidence to be collected.

Select several students to be the investigative team. Identify each of them with such roles as chief investigator, investigator, or lab technician. Provide the investigative team with an evidence kit, which is described below.

Excitement could be added to the mini Crime Scene Investigation by setting it up so that a student of yours is a witness and has some information to provide. However, remember to keep this investigation simple because it is just practice for the actual Crime Scene Investigation.

To help this activity seem more realistic, you may have a police officer bring in shirts, jackets, hats, and so on, so the investigative team can "dress up." This can be a lot of fun. Be sure to take pictures!

As the investigative team members proceed from station to station, they will use proper procedures to collect the physical evidence. You or one of your experts may want to follow the team through the stations to assist and explain to the class the hows and whys of collecting physical evidence.

To get the whole class involved, you may want to provide a piece of physical evidence to the entire class to compare to evidence from the suspect. However, as you design this activity, keep in mind that it is a simple practice activity to build interest and skills for the actual Crime Scene Investigation. HAVE FUN!

Evidence Kits

During this time, prepare the evidence kit, which can be used in preparation activities before going to the library to collect actual physical evidence. The following is a suggested list of what the kit should include (one kit for each investigative team).

Suggested Materials for Evidence Kit:

✓ One gallon-size plastic bag
✓ One lunch-size paper bag
✓ Three plastic sandwich bags
✓ One pair of plastic gloves
✓ Masking tape to seal bags and be signed by investigative team
    member

Make these kits available to students when they go to the library to collect the physical evidence from the crime scene. Kits should be kept and stored in the classroom.

ENGLISH PRELIMINARY ACTIVITIES

The skills your students use in the Crime Scene Investigation are ones that are used in the classroom throughout the school year. Students will practice listening, speaking, reading, and writing skills.

The Writing Process

You may want to have your students write a sample news article about a current event in local, state, or international news. Have them use the four-step writing process: clustering/mapping, writing the rough copy, editing, and writing the final copy. Have them focus on the facts of the article. This will be good practice for the crime scene article and will serve as a model.

Writing a Scene

Have students use the characters from a familiar story or novel and write a scene of dialogue. There are many mystery and suspense stories in student anthologies. Select one and have students change the narrative to a dialogue. They may extend the story and write a sequel.

Making Predictions

Students may use their daily journals to predict the ending of a story or novel. Have them record details and clues that foreshadow what they think may happen. These predictions will help students focus on details the author uses.

Role-Playing

You may have your students role-play characters from a story or novel. Is their interpretation of the character the same as the author's? Have the students discuss this activity. They may create a new character. How would this change the plot?

You might also create a scene in class in which some kind of crime happens—for example, a backpack is taken. Have students act out the scene. Have the rest of the class write down what they saw as eyewitnesses. They should be specific and pay close attention to detail. The students may discover that there are many different versions of what happened. Which version is correct?

If you have access to a video camera, you might try the same activity and have someone tape the scene. After the students write their version, play the videotape for them to see how accurate their retelling is.

Peer Editing/Evaluation

After reading a story or a novel, have the students write a one-paragraph opinion. Have them pretend they are critics from the local newspaper. Did they like the work? Why or why not? Tell them to be specific. Have students work with a partner to edit each other's writing. Are there a topic sentence, details, and a conclusion? Did the writer use text from the book or story to support his or her opinion? Is the paragraph clear and concise? Have students correct usage and mechanics and work on a final copy.

HISTORY PRELIMINARY ACTIVITIES

Know Your Rights!

Your students will need to have a strong background in the United States Constitution, the Bill of Rights, and the remaining amendments to the Constitution. With these skills, your students will be more aware of the rights and responsibilities of the suspects/defendants as well as those of the government.

The Constitution

When you study the Constitution, focus on the powers granted to the federal government. What are the three branches of government? What are their responsibilities? Those are two questions you will want to ask your students continually as you pursue your study.

The Bill of Rights and Miranda Rights

The Bill of Rights will be a fascinating study for you and your students. These 10 amendments will be the key to the success of the investigations and to the trial itself. Carefully study what individual rights citizens of the United States are guaranteed. Such ideas as the Miranda rights (chapter 16), search and seizure, attorneys present for questioning, subpoenas, and search warrants should be discussed as you lead your class through this most amazing document. Be sure students know what they can and cannot do as players in this trial pertaining to the Bill of Rights.

Constitution Curriculum

Many publishers have some outstanding Constitution curricula that you might use. Try some of the interactive activities that some publishers offer. Be sure that it is designed for all levels of ability in your classroom. ***REMEMBER, ALL ABILITY LEVELS CAN PARTICIPATE IN THIS PROJECT!*** You might even create your own curriculum to use during this study.

The study of the Constitution, the Bill of Rights, and other amendments will be rewarding for you. You will see your students begin to relate this study to their everyday lives. Once students have learned about the Constitution and the Bill of Rights, they can begin to think about which role they would like to assume in the upcoming courtroom procedure.

How do they know what job to apply for in the trial? Check out "Students Apply for Courtroom Jobs" (chapter 14) and find out!

 # SUGGESTIONS FOR STUDENTS WITH SPECIAL NEEDS

Below is a list of suggestions that can be used to help your students with special needs. Adapt and change the activity as needed to best meet the needs of your students.

- Group students into teams to work together on preparation activities.

- Provide completed samples of forms so students can compare and check to see that they are correctly completing the assignment.

- During science lab time, allow time to discuss what they have described and discovered and what it means.

- Provide time before or after school for assistance and make-up lessons.

- Have classroom aides monitor the progress of individuals.
- Modify expectations for some students.
- Assign courtroom duties related to ability level.
- Select literature appropriate for each level.
- Modify the writing assignments for each level.
- Pair up students of low ability with more capable students.

By adapting and changing the activity, you can provide a rewarding experience to all of your students.

Chapter Four

Preparation of Evidence

This Crime Scene Investigation takes place in the school library. Students have displayed their collections of sports cards and antique dolls. The next morning it is discovered that the display in the library has been broken into and most of the collections have been stolen.

MATERIALS NEEDED FOR THE CRIME SCENE

To set up the crime scene in the library, here is a list of materials you will need to have in advance (figure 4-1). You may want to have these materials organized in one carry box for ease of setting up and dismantling in the library.

1. Four to five dolls. These could be purchased from secondhand stores, or you could ask students for old dolls. These dolls should have plenty of long hair, so that samples may be cut.

2. Twenty to thirty sports cards. Any type will suffice for this crime scene.

3. One roll of yellow caution tape. Construction caution tape or police line tape (ask the local police department) will work best.

4. Microscope slides or glass plates/mirrors (two per team of four students). These will be used for fingerprints. As explained later in this chapter, you will prepare the slides with fingerprints that the students will discover and use as evidence. Make sure the edges are safe and not sharp. Caution students on their proper use and handling.

5. Inked shoe print on notebook paper. One original found in library, one photocopy for each student.

6. Handwritten note. One original found in library, one photocopy for each student. The note might say:
    "Let's meet together after school to divide up the things we get."

7. Scissors for cutting hair.

8. Masking tape for taping the yellow caution tape to create a police line.

9. Cards for numbering evidence stations. One for each station (folded in half so that they stand and can be seen easily).

10. A camera.

TEACHER PREPARATION PRIOR TO SETTING UP IN THE LIBRARY

To save time and for an easy and fast setup of the crime scene, have the necessary materials ready in advance. To make the Crime Scene Investigation as realistic as possible, you may want to have an actual collection on display for several days. The easier option is just to tell the students that the display was set up the day of the crime and what they will actually see will be the crime scene with the remaining pieces and the physical evidence of the crime.

On the day the students are told the Crime Scene Investigation story line, remember it is their imaginations that carry the story away into an exciting, student-centered activity. As the investigation progresses, you will be surprised at the suspects and explanations they develop to explain the crime scene.

When reading the explanations of how to set up and organize the physical evidence in the library, remember to adapt and change the activity as needed to adjust to your physical setting and needs.

Police Line

Using the yellow police line/construction caution tape to create a police line around the crime scene helps give it a realistic appearance. Create a police line around the crime scene and anywhere else you feel is necessary in the library to ensure its integrity. The police line you create will also help the flow of your students as they move from station to station collecting the physical evidence.

Doll Evidence

After the crime scene has been set up and students have been told a crime has taken place, they will find that one or two dolls have been left behind in the library. It is suspected that the thieves may have handled and tossed down the dolls. If, in fact, the suspects did do this, then it is possible that the suspects may have doll hair fibers on their clothing.

To check for these fibers, students will be cutting a few doll hair fibers for each team member. These hair fibers will be compared to hair fibers that have been found on the suspects.

You will need to decide which dolls will be left behind at the crime scene in the library. These dolls should have plenty of long hair so the investigative teams can cut samples and bag them for later analyses and comparisons. The remaining dolls will be used later to cut hair fibers. These fibers will be provided to students in the crime lab as hair fibers found on the suspects. Hair from the dolls in the library will be cut by you later and provided to students as evidence taken from one or more of the suspects. In this way one or two of the suspects will have a match to the dolls' hair found in the library.

Sports Card Evidence

Sports cards are a part of the display in the library. After the crime has taken place, 20 to 30 sports cards will be found scattered around in the library. This scenario helps to make the crime look more realistic, as if someone had taken the cards and scattered the rest. Sports cards are not actually used as part of the physical evidence. However, if you wish, you could substitute this evidence for one of the other pieces of evidence or also use the sports cards as one more additional piece of evidence.

Suspects could be found with sports card on them. An "inventory list" could show that those cards that were found on the suspects were also part of the display. Adapt, change, and use this piece of evidence to best meet your individual needs.

Fingerprint Evidence

While the crime was taking place in the library, it is suspected that items were touched and fingerprints were left behind. It is suspected that the display cases were probably touched as they were broken into, thus leaving fingerprints on the glass.

The microscope slides, glass plates, and mirrors represent the broken parts of the display cases. Each team will take two glass plates to check for fingerprints in the crime lab.

To prepare the glass plates, you will need to put your right thumbprint on each glass plate at least twice. This print will now be the print of one of the suspects. You will later use your right thumbprint again to print the suspect's thumbprint to be used as evidence.

When printing so many of your thumbprints on so many glass plates, it will be helpful to use a small amount of grease or oil on your right thumb. You will want to experiment a little to see what works best for you.

When you use a little grease or oil, it is easy to see a clear fingerprint on the glass, making it easier for the students to see the fingerprint.

We have tried a variety of materials, from hair care products to machine grease found in the stockroom. We have found the thicker the better, and a little is all you will need.

Remember to provide rounded glass edges and have students use caution, as always, in handling the microscope slides.

Shoe Print Evidence

As your investigative teams enter the library, they will notice a piece of paper on the floor with a shoe print on it. Your investigative teams will probably ask how it is possible that a shoe print is left behind. Nearby, you may want to set poster paints or ink that was used to make signs for the display. One of the bottles could be spilled on a sign board; a suspect has stepped into the ink and then stepped on a piece of paper. Students' love of mystery makes it all very real for them.

A few days before setting up the crime scene, you will need to decide if you want boots or another type of shoe. Find some volunteers to come in after school to make some shoe prints. You will need one print for the library and three different prints for the three suspects. It works well to have one suspect's print match the evidence print and a second suspect's print similar to but not a match of the one left behind in the library.

Do not make the shoe print too easy for the investigative teams. When you have decided which shoe print to use, you will need to make two prints of it. One print is the one found in the library. Make enough photocopies for everyone.

Make a second print of the same shoe so that it will match the suspect's print. Make this print challenging to match by turning the paper to a different angle and by applying a different amount of pressure when pressing down on the paper. This will make the prints similar yet different enough that the defense attorneys can argue that the two prints are definitely not the same. The trial becomes more interesting if you leave a little bit of doubt occasionally in the evidence.

To make the print, we have found that ink from an ink pad brushed on the bottom of the shoe and then pressed down on paper works well. Stepping on paper several times helps to clean the ink off. Finish cleaning by rubbing a cloth on the inked parts of the shoe.

Once a student volunteer did not clean off the bottom of his shoe. When he walked down the hall, he left a trail of prints in the direction of the library. We thought it would be gone by the next day.

The next day, science classes went to the library to collect physical evidence. Returning to class, I found my students scattered up and down the hallway drawing, tracing, and trying to match the shoe prints. The investigative teams asked if this was part of the evidence! This was not a planned part of the Crime Scene Investigation, but unexpectedly a new dimension was added. Change and adapt as you need to your setting and situation.

Number of Shoe Prints Needed

Library

✓ One original print found in the library
✓ Photocopies of original print for students

Suspects
✓ Photocopies of suspect print that matches library print
✓ Photocopies of second suspect's shoe print
✓ Photocopies of third suspect's shoe print

Cloth Fiber Evidence

Before setting up the evidence in the library, you will need to find three or four different types of cloth to use in the crime scene. When students are introduced to the crime scene, they will be told that it appears a suspect may have snagged his or her shirt on the corner of a table and has thus left cloth fibers there.

Old shirts work well. Selecting materials that are similar makes later comparisons more challenging. Selecting materials that are too different may make it too easy for comparison. To prepare the fibers, cut the material into small patches (about two by two inches). Pull out and separate the individual threads. A minimum of three different materials will need to be prepared. Bag up each separate cloth material to be used later in the investigation. Each student will need to collect two to three fibers at the crime scene.

One of the three cloth samples will be left behind at the crime scene, and the investigative teams will collect and bag about two to three fibers for each team member.

Later, back in the lab, the investigative teams will be provided with cloth fibers found in the library that will match those of one suspect. The other two suspects' cloth fibers will not match those found in the library.

Handwritten Note Evidence

Once investigative teams go to the crime scene, they will be told that a handwritten note was found in the area. The note says:

Let's meet together after school to divide up the things we get.

You may want to use this note or write your own. This type of note allows for different interpretations later in the courtroom trial. A more specific note could be more incriminating to one of the suspects. The handwriting on the notes should be unfamiliar to the students. Do not be surprised when your students start asking you and your team teachers for handwriting samples!

In the library you will need the original note (tape it down on the table) and one photocopy of the original for each team member.

35

Fig. 4-1. Crime Scene Evidence

Science

Library—Stolen collection of dolls and collectible sport cards

witnesses
- one witness establishes what was in the library and the presence of suspicious-looking people
- second witness heard a noise and saw people leaving the library

hair samples
- hair fibers taken from doll collection

fingerprints
- fingerprints on broken display case

shoe print
- shoe print left on sheet of paper

cloth fibers
- torn fibers on corner of bookcase

diagrams/ maps
- map out where evidence was found and where entrances and exits are located

writing sample
- note left behind—evaluated in English class

Chapter Five

Setting Up the Crime Scene

Once you have taken the time to prepare the physical evidence, setting up the crime scene only takes a little time. The library should be set up the afternoon before the students are to make their first visit to interview the witnesses.

The second visit to the library will be to collect the physical evidence. In setting up the crime scene, consider the following items:

- Have all evidence readily available to students as they rotate from station to station.

- Station number cards should be easily visible at each evidence location.

- Police line yellow tape helps the flow of students through the crime scene area.

- Spread evidence out over a large area so each investigative team will have plenty of room to work.

- Leave enough tables available for students to sit at and work.

- Think about how the investigative teams will circulate through the numbered evidence stations.

- Prepare a diagram of how you want the crime scene to look.

- Adapt and change as needed.

- Have extra supplies available in the library to use as needed.

CREATING THE CRIME SCENE

Locate the station number cards throughout the library where the evidence will be located. This will help you to see and to judge the spacing of the evidence. Here is a suggested list of station numbers for the evidence:

Station 1—Fingerprints
Station 2—Doll Hair
Station 3—Handwritten Note
Station 4—Cloth Fibers
Station 5—Shoe Print
Station 6—Another piece of evidence, such as second doll or mapping station
Station 7—Mapping Station
Station 8—Mapping Station

Fingerprints

The fingerprint station will have the microscope slides and glass plates with at least two thumbprints on each plate. Spread the plates out at this station so they are available to students. Remind students or have an instruction card at the station reminding students to handle the glass carefully. This evidence needs to be placed in a paper bag. Students should not handle the plates while they are in the paper bags or the fingerprints may be erased.

Doll Hair

The doll hair station will have a doll that has been left behind and a pair of scissors to cut a hair sample. Having one doll for evidence works well. A second doll can be used if you wish. Remind the students or have an instruction card at the station reminding students to cut one to two hair fibers for each team member. Hair fibers should be placed in plastic sandwich bags from the team evidence kit.

Handwritten Note

The handwritten note station will have the original note taped to the table. Remind the students or have an instruction card at the station reminding students to make one photocopy of the handwritten note for each investigative team member. The copies can be placed in the large, gallon-sized plastic bag.

Cloth Fibers

The cloth fiber station will have the previously prepared cloth fibers spread out over a table or counter. Remind the students or have an instruction card reminding students to take two to three fibers for each investigative team member. This evidence can be placed in a plastic sandwich bag from the crime kit.

Shoe Print

The shoe print station will have the previously prepared shoe print original and a photocopy for each student. The original copy should be taped to the floor. Some poster boards and bottles of ink can be placed around it on the floor. Students can be told that custodians have cleaned up spilled ink and other debris and have left the evidence for the investigation. Remind students or have an instruction card reminding students to take one copy for each investigative team member. These copies can be placed in the large, gallon-sized plastic bag.

Other Evidence

To adapt and change the activity to your special circumstances, you may want to provide additional pieces of evidence.

Mapping Station

While collecting the physical evidence from the crime scene, the students also need to draw a map of the library. The map should show major features of the library and locations of where the pieces of evidence were collected. As the students rotate through the stations, several tables should be designated where they can sketch a draft of the library for later use in making a final drawing. Included here is a sample diagram of what the students may want to draw (figures 5-1 and 5-2).

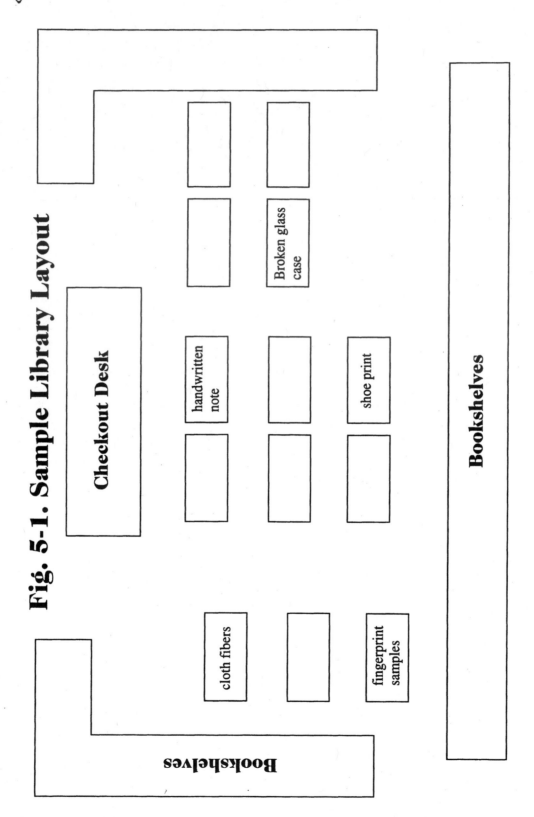

Fig. 5-1. Sample Library Layout

Checkout Desk

Bookshelves

Bookshelves

handwritten note

Broken glass case

shoe print

cloth fibers

fingerprint samples

Fig. 5-2. Student

Map of Crime Scene

Location: _____

Investigating Officer: _____

Date: _____

Time: _____

The Witnesses

Check with your witnesses the day before your investigative teams go to the library to make sure your witnesses know their stories. You may want to provide them with a written script or outline to follow. The general story line for the witnesses is described in chapter 1. These witnesses should be teachers, administrators, or counselors who could give a day to be interviewed, which helps involve the school community.

One witness will explain that he or she saw the displays being set up by the students and that the displays included antique dolls and sports cards. The second witness will explain that he or she heard a loud noise and saw students running from the library. This witness may be able to identify the suspects. It works well if the witnesses are specific on some details and vague on others. With both concrete and vague information, the attorneys will have more to debate in court and it will not be an open-and-shut case.

READY TO START

The evidence has been prepared, the library has been set up, the witnesses know their stories, and the students have practiced how to interview and collect physical evidence.

The *first day* the students visit the library will be in their English classes. On this day, they will see the crime scene but will only interview the witnesses. Don't let the witnesses just tell their stories. The students should be called upon to ask questions and discover what happened, with details. This part of the crime investigation should take one class period for each class.

On the *second day*, the science classes will have the opportunity to visit the crime scene. The student investigative teams will be reminded to collect, bag, and label all physical evidence properly. Collecting of the physical evidence and diagramming of the library will take one class period for each class. Before taking your science class to the library, make sure you have considered the following suggested instructions:

1. Properly handle all physical evidence.
2. Properly bag all physical evidence.
3. Properly label all physical evidence bags with masking tape.
4. Map major library features and where physical evidence was collected.
5. Make sure all team members sign a chain of custody (explained in the next chapter) when collecting physical evidence.

Chapter Six

Collecting and Analyzing Evidence

The evidence has been prepared, the crime scene has been set up, and now is the time for the students to visit the crime scene and to collect evidence.

43

FIRST-DAY INTERVIEWS

On the first day students from the English classes will be visiting the crime scene. They have studied and practiced their interviewing skills and are now ready to put them to use.

Once you are in the library, explain or review the basics of when and where the crime took place. Introduce each witness separately and provide the students with time to interview each one.

SECOND-DAY COLLECTING OF PHYSICAL EVIDENCE

On the second day, the science classes visit the crime scene to collect the physical evidence. Once you are in the library, review with them how to collect the physical evidence and how to bag and label the evidence properly. Remember to have investigative team members sign their chain of custody papers (see explanation below) after collecting the physical evidence.

The investigative teams should be rotated through the crime scene stations. The students need approximately four to five minutes at each station.

HOW TO ANALYZE AND REPORT PHYSICAL EVIDENCE

Once the physical evidence has been collected, several class sessions will be spent analyzing and evaluating the physical evidence. Each member of the investigative teams should write his or her own report and all related crime scene information. Diagrams and reports should be organized into each student's portfolio.

Each piece of evidence should be evaluated and reported separately. One to two days in the science classroom should be provided to evaluate each separate piece of physical evidence. On every day that a new piece of evidence is to be evaluated, instructions and suggestions should be provided to the students.

CHAIN OF CUSTODY

Each time the plastic bag containing the physical evidence is opened, each investigative team member must sign, date, and record the time on the chain of custody sheet (figure 6-1). When the physical evidence is returned to the evidence bag, the chain of custody sheet must be signed again by each team member who has worked with the physical evidence.

The chain of custody is a record of who has handled the physical evidence and when this handling took place. There must be no break in the chain of custody. Evidence must always be accounted for. The chain of custody is a legal document that can be used in the trial. If the chain of custody is not properly handled, then the evidence can become questionable and thus can be thrown out of court.

When evidence is checked out to the investigative team members to include in their portfolios, it becomes evidence to be used in the trial. It should be noted on the chain of custody that is has been checked out for that purpose. Each investigative team member should have a copy of the chain of custody in his or her portfolio.

PHYSICAL EVIDENCE REPORT

For each piece of physical evidence evaluated, a physical evidence report should be completed (figure 6-2). The type of physical evidence and a description of its physical characteristics are listed on the report. A careful description of the physical evidence will be helpful in the trial.

During lab time, you will provide to the investigative teams the evidence taken from the three suspects. The teams then have an important task to complete: They must compare the evidence left behind at the scene of the crime to the evidence taken from the suspects to see if there is a match. Under "COMPARISON OF CRIME EVIDENCE TO SUSPECT EVIDENCE" on the physical evidence report, the investigative team members should report either how the evidence from the crime scene and the evidence from the suspects are different or if there is a match between the two.

The final part of the physical evidence report is for the students to tape the actual evidence in the space provided under "CRIME SCENE EVIDENCE." The evidence should include the evidence taken from the crime scene as well as the evidence taken from the three suspects. This report is now evidence that can be used in the trial.

MATCHING UP THE EVIDENCE

During the time spent in the lab analyzing and matching up the physical evidence, it is important to start identifying the suspects. The suspects could be identified at this time by one of two methods; they could be identified by names that you provide or as suspects A, B, and C.

It works best for all of your classes if you provide the suspects with fictitious names that all classes will use and that will also be used in the trial. Pick the names you would like to use in the trial. For purposes of description, we will identify them at this time as suspects A, B, and C.

When you provide the physical evidence from the suspects to the investigative teams, you must consider the match and how much evidence there will be against each suspect. Here is an evidence match you may want to use:

Witness can identify all three suspects running from library.
>
> Fingerprint—Matches suspect B
> Hair from doll—Matches suspect A
> Shoe print—Matches suspect C
> Cloth fibers—Matches suspect A
> Handwriting—Matches suspect B

You may want to have the evidence from the suspects in plastic bags labeled "A," "B," and "C." During lab time, allow the students to obtain the physical evidence and compare it for possible matches.

Fig. 6-1. Chain of Custody

Name	Date	Description of what was checked out	Checked out	Returned
1.				
2.				
3.				
4.				
5.				
6.				
7.				
8.				
9.				
10.				
11.				
12.				
13.				
14.				
15.				
16.				
17.				
18.				
19.				
20.				
21.				
22.				
23.				
24.				
25.				
26.				
27.				
28.				
29.				
30.				
31.				
32.				
33.				

Fig. 6-2. Physical Evidence Report

Evidence: _____

Description: _____

_____

_____

_____

_____

_____

_____

_____

Comparison of crime evidence to suspect evidence: _____

_____

_____

_____

Crime scene evidence: (attach actual evidence)

This is a good time to mention to students that this is a real test of their scientific investigative skills. Not only will they be using these skills in the science lab, but these skills will also be called upon in the courtroom as they testify as experts on the different pieces of physical evidence.

Checklist of Suggested Materials Needed in the Crime Lab:

✓ Microscopes
✓ Hand lenses
✓ Fingerprint dusting materials
✓ Clear tape
✓ Physical evidence reports
✓ Suspect evidence

Suggested time allotment for each crime lab period:

- **5 to 10 minutes:** Special instructions reminding them which piece of evidence is to be worked on and what to look for.
- **30 to 40 minutes:** Student working time.
- **5 minutes:** Clean-up.

One day should be used for each piece of physical evidence. It is also suggested that you have one day as a "make-up" day for students to catch up on and finalize their reports. During the crime lab time, you may want to consider the following:

- Arrange for extra time before or after school to provide more individual instruction for students.

- Make sure that students are working together in their investigative teams.

- Check to see that other team teachers are providing class time and instruction in evaluating physical evidence.

- At the start of each crime lab period, give an example of how to describe and compare.

- Have a large, poster-size example of a completed physical evidence report.

- Have aides or volunteer helpers in the classroom to assist you.

Chapter Seven

Crime Scene Portfolio

The crime scene portfolio includes all the work done in the three subject classes: science, English, and history. It also includes a final evaluation of the activity written by the students. This evaluation allows them to write their opinions of the project, to tell you what they learned, and to offer suggestions. The portfolio is the end product of many weeks of work. The students will feel a great sense of pride and accomplishment in what they have done. A sample layout of the portfolio is provided on the next page.

TABLE OF CONTENTS

I. Description of Crime

II. Science
1. Chain of custody
2. Map of library
3. Fingerprint report
4. Cloth/thread report
5. Hair report
6. Shoe print report

III. English
1. Interview questions
2. Writing the news article I
3. Writing the news article II
4. Writing the news article III
5. Mystery story report
6. Reading a mystery novel
7. Writing a mystery story
8. Police report
9. Handwriting comparison

IV. History
1. Job application
2. Student research and written job descriptions
3. Explanation of jobs—see chapter 14.

V. Student Evaluation

STUDENT EVALUATION

Writing an evaluation gives students an opportunity to look back over many weeks of work and assess what they have done. They will have participated in cooperative learning activities, role-playing, individual assignments, and working with a partner. The evaluation and portfolio are final activities that can show their work as an example of growth over time.

Areas to Consider

Here are some suggested questions and topics for students to address in their evaluations:

1. What is your overall impression of the project?
2. What specific things did you like?
3. Was there any part of the project that you did not like? Explain.
4. What did you learn from this project?
5. How would you change the project to make it better?
6. What advice would you give to students about to begin the Crime Scene Investigation?

Chapter Eight

Interviewing the Witnesses

The first step in the English portion of the project is to interview the witnesses of the crime. The students will visit the crime scene, this time as objective observers, to ask questions and to gather facts. Ask them to imagine themselves (or role-play) as a reporter. Their newspaper has sent them to cover the story of the crime. The community is upset about the break-in at the school library. The students will need to gather the facts. Their questions should be specific and direct. They may not get the opportunity again to talk to these witnesses. The students will use the answers to their questions in their news stories. They may also come across evidence that will be important in the trial.

Here are some suggested questions for the students to ask the witnesses:

1. What is your name, address, and occupation?
2. Why were you at the crime scene?
3. What time/day were you at the scene?
4. Describe what you saw in the library.
5. Did you see anyone?
6. If so, what was the person(s) doing? Any suspicious behavior?
7. Try to describe the person(s):
    Age?
    Clothing?
    Physical characteristics?
    Any unusual features (scars, etc.)?
    Carrying objects?
8. Did you see anyone else in the area who may also be a witness?
9. Describe what the suspects were doing.
10. Did you speak to them? Explain.
11. Was there anything suspicious said?

DESCRIPTION OF THE CRIME

It is helpful for the students to write a brief description of the crime after they have visited the crime scene, interviewed the witnesses, and collected the physical evidence. A Description of Crime form is provided for you to copy and have your students use (figure 8-1). The description is brief and should be placed in the front of the students' portfolios.

Fig. 8-1. Description of Crime

When: _____

_____

_____

_____

Where: _____

_____

_____

_____

_____

Description: _____

_____

_____

_____

_____

_____

_____

_____

_____

_____

Chapter Nine

Writing the News Article

In order for students to understand how to write their own articles, they first need to look at a real news story as a model.

Have each student bring in a news article from the newspaper. You may want to have them work with a partner to have more than one article to compare. Have them clip out the article and staple it to their newspaper article evaluation form (figure 9-1).

Fig. 9-1. Newspaper Article Evaluation Form

Name of newspaper: _____

_____

Date: _____

Headline: _____

_____

What happened? _____

_____

_____

Who was involved? _____

_____

_____

_____

Where did this happen? _____

_____

_____

_____

Why? _____

_____

_____

How? _____

_____

_____

Quotes (from witnesses, police, etc.): _____

_____

_____

_____

Briefly summarize the article (on back):

ELEMENTS OF A NEWS ARTICLE

The students will have the opportunity to see the six elements of a news article—who, what, when, where, why, and how—in an example they have brought from home. If the students are working with a partner, have them do the same questions, answers, and summary for the second article. You may ask them to write or discuss which article contained more facts, or which one appeared to be better written.

They will use these models in writing their own news stories.

CRIME SCENE ARTICLE

The students are now ready to write their own news stories based on the crime scene. Ask them once again to imagine that they are reporters. They have the assignment to write the breaking story about a school theft. They have been to the library, have interviewed the witnesses, and have all the facts they need to begin. They need to use as much detail as they can in their stories. Their job may depend on it!

Have students cluster their information as follows:

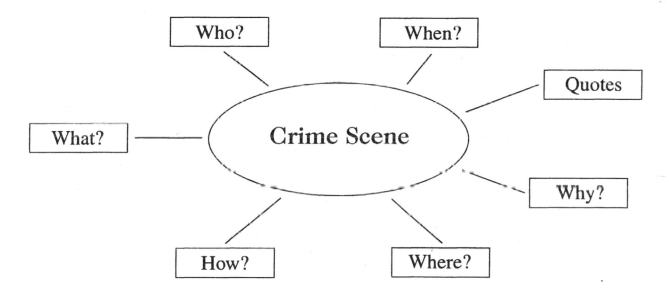

This will give them a visual image as well as a way to organize the facts.

Tell the students to write a rough draft of the article including the following information (figure 9-2):

- Headline
- Byline
- Date
- Who?
- What?
- When?
- Where?
- Why?
- How?
- Quotations from witnesses or police officers

THE EDITING PROCESS

Once your students have written their first copy, have them work with a partner to edit the article. They should check for the essential information as well as for usage and mechanics. Tell them they are now critics of each other's work. They need to look for ways to improve each other's writing.

WRITING THE FINAL COPY

After all necessary corrections are made, each student should prepare his or her final copy. If your school has a computer lab, have the students type the article in the lab. This will give the students a chance to work on word processing skills. Stress to them that corrections and improvements should be made until the final copy is turned in.

WRITING THE NEWS ARTICLE

Here is an opportunity for your students to see if their writing is of professional quality. Have them compare the news article they wrote with the one they analyzed from the newspaper.

Here are some suggested questions:

1. Have you answered all of the factual questions?
2. Do you have quotations from police, witnesses, and so forth?
3. Does you article contain a topic sentence, details, and a conclusion?
4. How does your article compare with the one from the paper? Which one do you think is better? Why?

You may have them include a drawing or a photograph with their articles.

Fig. 9-2. News Article Worksheet

Who: _____
_____
_____
_____

What: _____
_____
_____
_____

When: _____
_____
_____
_____

Where: _____
_____
_____
_____

Why: _____
_____
_____
_____

How: _____
_____
_____
_____

Chapter Ten

Police Report

The police and evidence reports are important part of the Crime Scene Investigation. Here is a way for you to call upon the community. Have a school resource or community police officer come into your class and talk to the students about how reports are filed. Students must listen carefully to instructions, pay close attention to details, and fill out detailed forms.

Students will see the importance of writing skills in the real world because an actual police report can be many pages long.

THE REPORT

The following forms are sample police and evidence reports. The students will fill in all the information about the library theft. They can then re-create the crime in a one-paragraph summary at the end. This report will be important for the trial. Have students work in pairs or small groups to check each other's work along the way. You may want to work on one form each day.

The included forms are:

- Police Report (figure 10-1)
- Property Report (figure 10-2)
- Evidence Collected Report (figure 10-3)

Fig. 10-1. **Police Report**

Investigating Officer: _____

Date: _____ Case Number: _____

Location of crime: _____

Date: _____ Time crime occurred: _____

Victim(s) name(s): _____

Occupation: _____

Other related information: _____

_____

_____

Description of what happened: _____

_____

_____

_____

_____

Description of crime area: _____

_____

_____

_____

_____

Description of how crime occurred: _____

_____

_____

_____

Were suspects arrested? _____

_____

Witnesses statements: _____

_____

_____

_____

_____

When possible, witnesses should sign initial written statements.
Use back of this paper if necessary.

Fig. 10-2. **Property Report**

Investigating Officer: _____

Date: _____ Case Number: _____

Page number: _____

The items listed below have been collected as evidence. This is your receipt that materials have been collected from:

Name/Location: _____

_____

_____

Date: _____ Time: _____

Item Number	Description of items. List each item separately.

Signature of Owner: _____

Date: _____

Investigating Officer: _____

Date: _____

Fig. 10-3. Evidence Collected Report

Investigating Officer: _____

Date: _____ Case Number: _____

Page number: _____

Item Number	Description of Item	Serial Number	Estimated Value

Vehicle (if involved): _____

Make: _____ Year: _____ License number: _____

Registered state: _____ Color: _____

General description: _____

_____

Date evidence was collected: _____

Who collected evidence: _____

Where evidence is stored: _____

Other information: _____

_____

_____

_____

_____

_____

Chapter Eleven

Handwriting Analysis

There was a note left behind at the crime scene. It is an important piece of evidence. It could solve the crime! Here is an opportunity for your students to put together clues as a detective would.

LIBRARY RESOURCES

Check out some books on handwriting analysis from your school library. Write a few generalizations on the chalkboard about basic handwriting styles. For example, some books state that people with large handwriting tend to be outgoing, while people with small handwriting are quiet and shy.

STUDENTS ANALYZE THEIR OWN STYLES

Have the students work with a partner. Write a sentence on the chalkboard for them all to copy. Using some generalizations about handwriting styles, have the students look carefully at their own writing and their partner's. What generalizations can be made? Are the books correct? Have them analyze your writing because they see it daily on the chalkboard. What conclusions can they make about you?

THE NOTE

Now that your students are experts in handwriting analysis, have them examine the crime scene note. What generalizations can be made about the suspect? Have the students profile the suspect in a paragraph. They will need to be very specific and pay close attention to details.

MATCHING THE SUSPECT'S WRITING

Ask three people at your school, including the person who wrote the crime scene note, to write a sentence on a piece of paper. Label the samples "A," "B," and "C." Hand out the papers to the students and ask them to match the writing on the crime scene note with the writing on the sample piece of paper. They may discover the match quickly, but they need to give specific reasons why the writing matches. Is it the slant? The size of the letters? Have them write one paragraph defending their answers.

Chapter Twelve

Literature: Writing a Mystery Story Group Activity

The Crime Scene Investigation lends itself to having students read and write a mystery story. Students can work in cooperative groups in science and history classes. Here is an opportunity to create a group story and have each student become an author.

STORY STARTERS

Story starters are a great way to get your students interested in writing. They can create characters, build a plot, and solve a mystery. You can have them work on this individually, in a cooperative group, with a partner, or as a class writing assignment.

The following story starters involve a mystery. Have the students illustrate their stories when they have finished writing. You may want to put them together in notebooks for a class collection of stories and put them on display.

Story Starter I

Detective Alicia got a telephone call at 4:00 p.m. from an anonymous caller warning of danger in the subway. She thought for a moment about the intricate subway system that spanned thousands of miles. She worried about the thousands of people who took the subway home during rush hour.

She needed to convince authorities of the danger and to shut down the subway before it was too late.

Have your students create a story that answers the following questions:

1. Who is the caller?
2. What is the danger?
3. How does Alicia come to the rescue?

Story Starter II

Wilson Middle School is shocked by a theft in the gym. After working months and months to raise money for new jerseys for the football team, Coach Harris and his team are devastated by the disappearance of the new jerseys.

Several of the boys were with the coach when he locked the gym at 5:00 p.m. The team had a game at 6:00 p.m., but because it was only a practice game, Coach Harris insisted that they wear their old jerseys and save the new ones for the first game of the season the next day.

After the practice game, the team and the coach returned to the gym. The boys left, and Coach Harris locked up.

When Coach Harris entered the gym the next day, the jerseys were gone.

Have your students create a story where they discover:

1. Why the jerseys were stolen.
2. Who stole them.
3. Whether the jerseys were recovered.

 73

Story Starter III

Detective Joe took a few days off to vacation at a nearby lake. He woke up early one morning to fish. After catching nothing for three hours, he felt a pull on the line. He thought he had caught a big one. While reeling in his catch, he began to notice many dead fish in the water. As he pulled up his line, he saw that he had caught nothing but a rusty car motor. As he looked closer at the water, he saw how badly polluted it was. What happened to the water? What was killing fish?

Have your students create a story in which they answer the following questions:

1. Why was the water polluted?
2. Was something in the community contributing to the pollution?
3. What steps did Detective Joe take to convince authorities to clean up the lake?

Story Starter IV

Have students work in a group of six or eight. Begin by giving the students a one- or two-line story starter. For example:

> *"It was a dark and stormy night when the detective entered the home. He saw broken glass . . . the lights went out . . . a crash was heard."*

Ask one of the students in each group to write a few lines continuing the story, keeping in mind the mystery theme. After five minutes, stop them. Have the students pass their papers to the next person in the group. Each person will continue writing the story on another student's paper.

This process goes on until everyone in the group has written on all the papers. Increase the time allowed so the students are able to read over the stories and think about what they want to say.

The last few lines written should end the story. Each writer should check that the story has a beginning, a middle, and an end.

Peer Editing Checklist:

Use the following list as a guide to edit your paper and your group's paper.

- ✓ topic sentence
- ✓ details
- ✓ conclusion
- ✓ capital letters
- ✓ spelling
- ✓ punctuation
- ✓ word choice (new and interesting vocabulary)
- ✓ sentence variety
- ✓ complete sentences
- ✓ awkward sentences
- ✓ verb tenses
- ✓ new paragraphs
- ✓ neatness
- ✓ grammar

READING THE STORIES ALOUD

When each group is finished, the stories should be read aloud to the class. Illustrations or a cartoon strip of the story can be added.

This activity works well in a computer lab. The students follow the same process, writing a line and changing computers to add to another's writing. They can simply change seats with others in the group and type the stories.

Each student has become an author. Every story is complete, and all students have been actively involved.

Chapter Thirteen

Reading a Mystery Novel Group Activity

The Crime Scene Investigation is a great way to get your students interested in reading a mystery novel. Because they role-play the part of detectives, they can look at a novel and see how the author creates a mystery, establishes suspense, and unravels the crime.

SCHOOL RESOURCES

Your school library may have many titles in the mystery genre. There are a wide variety of mystery novels available, depending on the ability level of your students. Ask the school librarian to set aside a table of books for your students. The librarian may also speak to the class about what titles and authors are available. More advanced readers may have a favorite author to bring in from home or the public library. This activity is a way to get students excited about reading. There are several mystery series that could captivate your students as well.

SUGGESTED ACTIVITIES

Here are some suggestions for your students. There are many ways to talk about a book. You may decide to assign an activity or to let them select the one they want to do.

1. Design a book cover for the book.
2. Create a collage.
3. Create a mobile.
4. Write a book review as a newspaper critic.
5. Give an oral report.
6. Write a scene of dialogue and select class members to act it out.
7. Create a video of the book.
8. Describe your favorite part.
9. Rewrite the ending.
10. Make a cartoon strip of important scenes.
11. Write 10 questions for an imaginary interview with the author.
12. Describe the ways the detective solved the crime.

LITERATURE: SHORT STORY

Reading a mystery or suspense story in English class is a way to keep the students' interest in the project extended to their other classes. There are many anthologies that contain excellent stories for students to read. The school librarian is a great resource for additional materials and suggestions beyond the classroom.

Suggested Questions

After the students read a story, have them work in small groups and answer the following questions:

1. What is the title of the work?
2. Who is the author?
3. Describe the detective or person who solved the mystery.

4. How was the crime solved?

5. What clues (foreshadowing) did the author give to help the reader solve the crime?

6. Write a brief summary (four or five sentences) of the story.

7. Were the methods the detective used to gather evidence similar to what you did in the Crime Scene Investigation? Explain.

As you can see, there is much flexibility built into this component of the Crime Scene Investigation unit, so that you can adjust this component to the ability level of your students. This activity is also a way in which the Crime Scene Investigation can get students interested in reading.

Chapter Fourteen

Students Apply for Courtroom Jobs

Now that the students have spent some time investigating, interviewing, filling out reports, and writing news stories, they have begun to develop a pretty good idea of the particular job that they would like to have in the upcoming trial. Remember also that the students are just coming off a study of the Constitution and the Bill of Rights. This is the part of the Crime Scene Investigation when they will begin their jobs for the trial.

JOBS INTRODUCED TO STUDENTS

Throughout the beginning stages of the Crime Scene Investigation, it is important for you to tell the students exactly what they are doing in their classes in relation to a particular job that they may want to do when it comes time for the trial. A list of courtroom and courtroom-related jobs should be posted on the board as follows:

- Prosecuting Attorneys
- Defense Attorneys
- Police Officers
- Courtroom Bailiffs
- Prosecution Criminologists
- Defense Criminologists
- Suspects
- Witnesses
- Court Reporters
- Court Clerk(s)
- Members of the News Crew
- Members of the Video Crew

The number of students for each job will depend on the size of your class. For example, you may have five or six attorneys and four or five criminologists. Students work for one side or the other—defense or prosecution. You will need to spend time giving a brief description of the responsibilities of each job and answering any questions that the students may have about the jobs.

Here is a sample of a few of the possible jobs that your students may apply for:

Court Clerk: Court clerks summarize what is taking place in the courtroom. They keep track of any of the judge's rulings, and at the end of the trial, they issue a list of all those rulings. Clerks mark all exhibits and evidence that come into the courtroom. They keep track of and label all evidence. Clerks assist the judge in anything the judge needs. A clerk is a judge's right hand. Clerks are the managers of the court and can have people arrested if they get out of hand. Clerks are spoken to as if one were speaking to the judge, because the clerk is the right-hand person of the judge.

Court Reporter: The court reporter takes notes on everything that is said in the courtroom as well as sneezes, sighs, coughs, and other noises. The reporter must take everything down. In criminal cases, a stenographic machine is used. In other cases, electronic media may be used.

Bailiff: The bailiff is responsible for bringing the defendants into the courtroom. He or she is also responsible for courtroom security and for making sure that the judge is protected at all times. The bailiff does a courtroom search in the morning and the afternoon. The bailiff is responsible for searching all persons entering the courtroom. He or she also acts as a "gopher" for the judge. The bailiff is responsible for the security of the jury. He or she must take members of the jury to lunch and accompany them outside of the courtroom.

Defense Attorney: The defense attorney must defend the defendant to the best of his or her ability. He or she must place reasonable doubt in the minds of the jury that the defendant committed the crime. The defense attorney has access to the prosecution witnesses and evidence. He or she must make sure that the constitutional rights of the defendant are protected.

Prosecuting Attorney: The prosecuting attorney works for the government. He or she must prove beyond a reasonable doubt that the defendant committed the crime. The burden of proof rests with the prosecution. The prosecutor has access to search warrants and the police to investigate all crimes. He or she has a difficult job in bringing all evidence to the court to prove the case beyond a reasonable doubt.

Criminologists: Criminologists are experts in their fields. They must have an answer or an explanation for even the smallest piece of evidence. They present scientific explanations for most of the evidence. Criminologists can be called to the witness stand by either the defense or the prosecution.

News Media: The news media must accurately report on the court proceedings to the public. Members of the media may be called as witnesses if they report on a sensitive area of the case. They use print media and electronic media to report the case.

Witnesses: Witnesses will testify to what they saw or heard in the library. Students will play the adult witness roles. Witnesses must learn the parts they are playing perfectly.

Suspects: Students will assume the roles of suspects. Suspects must learn their parts perfectly.

Police Officers: The police officers will work with the prosecution. They will also be the investigating officers of the crime.

STUDENTS FILL OUT JOB APPLICATIONS

Filling out job applications is an important part of the Crime Scene Investigation. For some students, this could be the first time they have filled out a job application. It is important that they use the utmost care when filling out this application. Let the students know that the neatness of this application could be the difference between getting a job and not getting one in the real world, and that this part of the project is important. Tell the students that neatness counts. They must fill out the form carefully.

On this application (figure 14-1), students will be applying for their first choice of job. Explain to them that, as in the real world, we do not always get our first choice. The same is true for the courtroom jobs. There are a limited number of job openings for this trial. With that in mind, let the students know that the criteria for the assignment of jobs will be neatness, job availability, ability to do the job, and class needs. On the bottom of the job application, have the students put down some second and third choices in case they don't get their first choice.

STUDENTS ASSIGNED JOBS

This is the part of the unit where you, the teacher, have to make some judgment calls. Using the criteria of neatness, job availability, personal ability to do the job, and the needs of the class depending on size, you assign the students to their jobs. This is a key part of the trial. You have to assess the ability levels of the students. The most difficult part of the trial and the success of the trial rests with the defense and prosecuting attorneys. You may want to look carefully at whom you select for these positions.

The day after they have turned in job applications, let the students know what their jobs are and then let them meet with their newly assigned groups. Go around to each group and let them know what you expect of them. The next step is to let the students research exactly what their jobs are going to be.

Fig. 14-1. Application for Employment

Social Security No.: _____

Last Name: _____ First Name: _____ Middle Name: _____

Address: _____ City: _____ Zip: _____ Phone: _____

How long have you lived at this address? _____

POSITION DESIRED: _____ SALARY DESIRED: _____

QUALIFICATIONS YOU HAVE FOR THIS JOB:

WHY SHOULD YOU BE HIRED FOR THIS POSITION OVER SOMEONE ELSE?

In case of emergency, notify: _____ Telephone: _____

Relationship: _____ Address: _____

Hobbies: _____

List special skills: _____

How many years of grammar school attended? _____ Name of grammar school: _____

List your sixth-grade classes and grades:

Please list three references that we can contact.

NAME	RELATIONSHIP	PHONE NUMBER
1.		
2.		
3.		

This organization does not discriminate on the basis of sex, race, age, physical or mental handicap, religion, or national origin.

AGREEMENT

I authorize investigation of all statements contained in this application. I understand that any false statements made as a part of this application will be considered sufficient cause for dismissal.

I consent to any and all medical examinations required by the hospital, and understand that if I am employed I will be on a probationary basis for three months from the date of employment.

_____

Signature

***Write down the name of TWO alternative jobs if your first choice is not available.

Chapter
Fifteen

Researching
the Job

In this section, students will research exactly what their jobs entail. You will need to use your school library or other resources. This is another opportunity for you to use community resources.

LIBRARY RESEARCH

You will need to plan beforehand with your school librarian or make other arrangements to get materials so your students can do a little checking up on what their jobs really are. Most school libraries have career encyclopedias or even career software available. Arrange with your librarian to have these materials available for use the day the students do their research.

This part of the unit is another perfect opportunity for you to use community resources. Invite people from the various areas to which the students have been assigned. Have a police officer, a member of the press, and an attorney come to visit your class to describe what their jobs entail.

Here is an outline of resources to help you out:

I. Library
    A. Career books
    B. Career encyclopedias
    C. Periodicals

II. Internet

III. Speakers
    A. Member of the news media
    B. Attorney
    C. Police officer
    D. Crime lab technician

Written Job Description

Once the students have had a chance to learn about their newly assigned jobs, they must now write job descriptions. The length should be about one page, but instruct your students to include the following:

- Describe the job as you understand it.

- What is the average salary of the job?

- What are the job responsibilities?

- What education level is required for this job?

- What are the reasons that you want this job?

For the students who have been assigned the roles of witness and suspect, it would be a little difficult to look up what their jobs are. When the other students are researching their jobs, these students should be practicing their new roles with some sort of script. It would be helpful to have the witnesses and suspects write out their role-plays and stories. Assessment of their job performance relies on how well they are at assuming these roles perfectly. You may want to meet with them to go over what their new scripts are. They must become great actors in these new roles.

The written job descriptions will become part of the Crime Scene Investigation portfolio.

Chapter Sixteen

Arrests and Trial Preparation

Now that the students know what their jobs are and what they believe to be their roles in the trial, it is time to begin preparing the prosecution case and the defense case.

CASE PREPARATION

Divide the students into two groups —the defense and prosecution. On the prosecution side, you will have the prosecuting attorneys, prosecution criminologists, police officers, and witnesses all working to put together the case against the suspects (defendants). On the defense side, you will have defense attorneys, defense criminologists, and suspects (defendants). The students who are a part of the news media will begin to learn how to operate the video camera and related equipment as available. The court clerk, court reporter, and bailiff(s) will begin to organize materials and equipment for the courtroom.

Prosecution Team

Have the prosecution team meet to select a lead attorney or one who will direct the plan of attack for the prosecution. If possible, have either a police officer, attorney, or judge meet with this group to give them some direction on how to proceed with the prosecution against the defendants and some tips on courtroom procedures.

Defense Team

Have the defense side meet as well. They will select someone to be in charge of the defense. Again, have this group meet with a police officer, defense attorney, or judge to give them some direction on how to proceed with a defense and some tips on courtroom procedures.

Criminologists

The criminologists are the lab technicians. The prosecution criminologists are the ones who would be working in the police crime lab. Assign each one of the prosecuting criminologists to be an expert in one of the areas of evidence: hair, fingerprints, cloth fiber, handwriting analysis, shoe prints. They will become the expert in that area, and when called to testify, they will be able to tie that particular piece of evidence to one of the defendants.

The defense criminologists will be assigned to the same areas of expertise as prosecution criminologists, but they will try to disprove the evidence tied to the defendants. They too must become experts in their fields.

Witnesses

The students who are assigned the role of witness will have to memorize a basic script, but they may add to it as they see fit. Be careful not to get too outrageous with the story. This is the same script that you will give to the "adult" witnesses who were interviewed by the students in chapter 8.

Here is an outline of the script:

Witness #1 (an adult)
- Left the library at the closing of school.
- Saw three students setting up the display:
    two boys
    one girl
- Display contained dolls and sports cards. Collection items were valued at approximately $2,500.
- Witness saw three people watching at other side of library. Could not identify clearly.
- Students said the librarian was supervising the setup of the display.
- Next morning, before school started, he or she noticed items missing. The display case was broken. Witness called police.

Witness #2 (an adult)
- Was in a room next to the library.
- About an hour after school closed, heard a crashing noise. Sounded like it was in the hallway. Went outside into hallway and saw three students running out of the library into the hallway:
    two boys
    one girl
- Yes, could identify them but does not know their names.
- They were wearing dark clothing, brown to dark hair, average height. Ran out of the library very fast.
- Called out for them to stop.
- Students ran out of the building; witness thought nothing more about it at the time.
- Students looked as if they were carrying some type of bag.

Two students will assume these roles. It is important that they know this script perfectly. It would be helpful also for these students to talk to the adult witnesses to find out what more they said in the interviews from chapter 8.

Suspects/Defendants

There are three suspects in this project. Therefore, there should be three students assigned as the suspects. There is some vital evidence that is linked to each of the three suspects.

Earlier, we called the suspects "A," "B," and "C." Now we will assign a name to them: suspects Anderson, Berry, and Chambers (a little unoriginal, but now we can remember who is who).

Suspect Anderson has the cloth fibers and hair fibers linked to him or her. Suspect Berry has the fingerprint and handwriting in the note linked to him or her. Suspect Chambers has the shoe print linked to him or her. These students must assume these roles and pieces of evidence, even if a real fingerprint is taken from suspect Berry. They must now assume the evidence that is linked to them.

PUTTING THE CASE TOGETHER

At this time, it may be helpful for all of your students to view a television show or movie that deals with a courtroom scene so that the students can get an even better idea of what procedures they should be using.

Now that the prosecution and defense teams have a direction and have elected a leader(s), they may begin to build their cases. Students at this point will rely on their newly learned skills of "individual's rights."

One thing that the prosecution team has working against it is the fact that it must prove "beyond a reasonable doubt" that the defendants did what they are charged with. The defense team must only plant reasonable doubt in the minds of the jurors that the defendants could not have committed the crime. It is a fine line; however, it is an important one that both teams must understand.

Search Warrants

According to the Bill of Rights, a person's property cannot be searched without a search warrant. Well, the Crime Scene Investigation even has this component (figure 16-1). If the prosecution team plans on doing any searches of the defendants' property or lockers, they must have a search warrant that has been issued by the acting judge. The acting judge is YOU! The prosecution team must submit a "Search Warrant Affidavit" (figure 16-2) to the acting judge. You will either approve or deny the affidavit.

This is a fun part of the Crime Scene Investigation. The students will really get into this part of the project. Only the prosecution team may request a search warrant. The defense team, however, is legally allowed to view any evidence that is obtained in a search.

One of the police officers must serve the search warrant, but the prosecution attorney(s) may be present for the investigation.

Before the search, the participating student *and* teacher will plant evidence linking the student to the crime. It is important that you (the teacher) monitor the searches that take place. Get permission from the participating students and inform them that the search can take place with their permission only, and you will be present during searches of lockers, backpacks, notebooks, and so forth. The students should be given ample warning of when the search will take place, allowing them time to remove any potentially embarrassing items from their lockers and other places. It is suggested that if you choose to do this as a part of your program that the student be present during the searches. Be sure the participating students are aware that they are a part of this planned portion of the investigation. At no time should individual students ever be searched.

Fig. 16-1. Search Warrant

Municipal court, _____Judicial district _____ ,

County of _____ vs. _____ Case No:_____

State of _____

THE PEOPLE OF THE STATE OF _____, to any sheriff, marshal, police officer, district attorney, investigator in the County of _____ . Proof by affidavit, having been this day made to me by _____ that there is probable cause for the issuance of a **SEARCH WARRANT** on grounds set forth in Penal Code Section 1524.

YOU ARE HEREBY COMMANDED to make a **SEARCH** at any time of the day, good cause having been shown therefore, of the following described persons or property:

In the County of _____, State of _____, for the following described property:

and articles of personal property tending to establish the identity of persons in control of the premises or vehicle to be searched, including the following: utility company receipts, rent receipts, canceled mail envelopes, and keys; and if you find the same or any part thereof, to retain the same in your custody subject to order of court as provided by law.

DATED this _____ day of _____, _____ .

_____

JUDGE OF THE MUNICIPAL COURT (Acting)

Fig. 16-2. Search Warrant Affidavit

IN THE MUNICIPAL COURT, _____JUDICIAL DISTRICT
COUNTY OF _____,
STATE OF _____

Your affidavit, personally appearing and being duly sworn, deposes and says that he has reason to believe that:

[　] on the property described here: [　] on the person of:

[　] in the vehicle described here:

(Describe the property, vehicle, person, to be searched)

UNDER OATH, AND DULY SWORN, WHAT PROBABLE CAUSE EXISTS FOR THIS SEARCH REQUEST:

UNDER OATH, AND DULY SWORN, WHAT IS EXPECTED TO BE FOUND IN THIS SEARCH:

_____

Signature   Date

The Arrests and Miranda Rights

The police officers actually need to arrest the suspects and read them their Miranda Rights. Here are the segments of the Miranda Rights:

1. *You have the right to remain silent. Do you understand this?*
2. *Anything you say may be used against you in court. Do you understand this?*
3. *You have the right to have an attorney present when you talk to me. Do you understand this?*
4. *If you want an attorney, but cannot afford one, an attorney will be appointed for you, at no cost to you, before questioning. Do you understand this?*
5. *Having these rights in mind, would you like to speak to me about this matter?*

At this point, the defense attorneys will take custody of the suspects (now defendants). It would be helpful at this point to see that each defendant has a defense attorney assigned to him or her.

Questioning the Suspects

Any questioning will be done in the presence of the suspects' attorneys. The police officers and a member of the prosecution team should question the suspects individually about their whereabouts at the time of the crime and other details. The questioning of suspects will take place during class time.

Notice to Appear

The Notice to Appear (figure 16-3) is used to call other students to the witness stand to either corroborate or to dispute the suspects' testimony. You can choose to allow students from other classes to be called up to the witness stand, or you can work with your own group of students. Prosecuting and defense attorneys—along with the teacher—develop the witness list.

COURTROOM PREPARATION

Have the bailiff(s), court reporter, and court clerk meet so that they may begin to organize (on paper) the courtroom setup. They must also make a list of any equipment that they may need for the trial.

The court reporter will need tape recording equipment to tape the entire proceedings. In the past, we have obtained recording equipment from our county courthouse. You might try to contact the presiding judge to see if this would be possible for you to do.

Fig. 16-3. Notice to Appear

County of _____.
State of _____.

_____ is hereby ordered to appear at the trial stated below:

Case Number 16753
People of the State of _____ vs. Defendants: _____
Superior Court of _____ County

Date:

Place:

Time:

_____

Acting Judge of the Superior Court

The court clerk (who is the right-hand worker of the judge) needs to make sure that all the evidence is packaged and prepared to be brought to trial. Any other evidence that is introduced in court will fall under the jurisdiction of the court clerk. When it is time for the verdicts to be read, the court clerk will perform this task. This student may want to contact a local court clerk to see what the correct procedure is for the reading of the verdicts.

The bailiff will be responsible for courtroom security of all parties, including the judge, the jury, the attorneys, the witnesses, the defendants, and the spectators. If you have access to handheld metal detectors, get them for the bailiffs to use during the trial. It makes them feel important. Bailiffs are also responsible for swearing in anyone who is testifying in court. Have these students contact a bailiff at the local courthouse to find out what the proper procedure is for the swearing in of people who are testifying.

It is best if you can hold the trial in a room larger than a classroom. If you have access to a school auditorium or multipurpose room, reserve it for three consecutive days. Meet with your stage manager or person responsible for audio equipment to have microphones set up for the trial. This is helpful for several reasons. One, the jury can hear everything clearly. Two, your audience can hear everything clearly. Three, the participants can hear each other clearly.

This will take some planning on your part. If you have a good stage manager, it will be a great help for you.

Following is a sample map of what the courtroom setup should look like (figure 16-4).

THE JUDGE

The judge is a very, very important part of the trial. It is helpful, but not necessary, to have someone who has a little courtroom experience. If possible, maybe someone on your staff could act as judge. Here is another chance to use community resources. Maybe a law student would serve as your judge. Maybe a judge would serve, or a police officer, or an attorney, or a parent with some legal background. Remember, the trial will last approximately three days.

THE JURY

You will need to organize a jury. A group of students from a different grade level would be best. All you need is 12 jurors, with a couple of alternates, for the duration of the trial. Have the jurors bring paper and pencil so they may make notes to themselves.

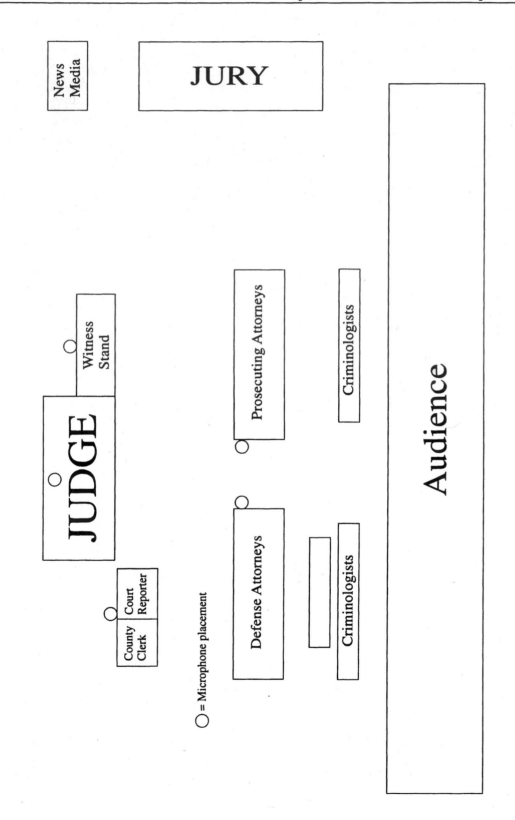

News Media

JURY

Witness Stand

JUDGE

Prosecuting Attorneys

Criminologists

Audience

County Clerk | Court Reporter

○ = Microphone placement

Defense Attorneys

Criminologists

Chapter Seventeen

The Trial

After weeks of hard work, the students reach a high point in the project, THE TRIAL. On the day(s) of the trial, require that the students dress appropriately for a courtroom setting. We have found that the students take this seriously and dress very nicely for the trial. Everyone should be dressed appropriately, from defendant to court reporter. At this point, you get to sit back and let the students take the trial on its course. You might offer some assistance to either the defense or the prosecution team. Other than that, just sit back and enjoy the results of your hard work.

CONDUCTING THE TRIAL

The following list is a step-by-step sequence for conducting the trial. The attorneys, judges, and police officers you consult can provide valuable details to make your trial realistic.

Opening Statements
- Prosecution
- Defense

Prosecution Case
- Police
- Witnesses
- Criminologists
    - Fingerprints
    - Cloth
    - Hair
    - Handwriting
    - Shoe Print

Defense Case
- Witnesses
- Criminologists

Closing Statements
- Prosecution
- Defense
- Prosecution

THE VERDICT

Once the trial is concluded, the jury will be taken into seclusion so that they may "deliberate" their decisions. You will need to go into the deliberations with the jury to give them some guidance on coming up with a decision. Have the members of the jury vote on their decision and then allow the group to try to convince those who might not agree.

Meanwhile, the rest of the students and the audience are on pins and needles waiting for the jury's decision. To make things interesting, have one of the bailiffs go to the judge during deliberations and request to see some piece of evidence or hear a portion of the audiotape of the trial. This makes everyone's anxiety jump sky-high. Again, direct the jury in arriving at a decision.

Once the jury has reached a verdict, have the bailiff tell the judge that the jury is ready to return. The judge will call the court to order and ask the jury to come into the courtroom. The jury will be seated, and the verdict will be handed to the judge for review. The judge will then hand the verdict to the court clerk, who will read the verdict. The judge will ask the defendants to rise. The court clerk must read one verdict at a time. The script could be as follows:

> *"We the jury, in the above entitled action, find the defendant*
> *_____ (Guilty/Not Guilty) for the crime*
> *of burglary in the first degree. On this ____ day of _____.*

Once the verdicts are read, the judge will ask the jury if this is their decision, and then dismiss them.

STUDENT EVALUATION/PORTFOLIO

The next day in class would be a good debriefing time for the students. Have the students do an evaluation of the entire project. This evaluation will become a part of the students' portfolios. We have provided a sample of a student evaluation for you to use (figure 17-1).

Fig. 17-1. Student Evaluation Form

1. What is your overall opinion of the Crime Scene Investigation?
   What did you like?

2. Would you like to do more interdisciplinary units in the future? Explain.

3. What were your roles in the Crime Scene Investigation?
   Science, English, History?

4. Has the Crime Scene Investigation influenced your thoughts of future career choices?
   Explain.

5. What kind of crime would you like to investigate in the future?

CIRCLE YOUR RESPONSE

6. How did you like solving a common team problem?

1	2	3	4	5
not at all				very much

7. Did you enjoy participating in the trial?

1	2	3	4	5
not at all				very much

8. Did you enjoy the mystery section?

1	2	3	4	5
not at all				very much

9. Did you enjoy collecting and analyzing the physical evidence?

1	2	3	4	5
not at all				very much

Chapter Eighteen

Creating Your Own Crime Scene

In the previous pages, you have been guided through the Crime Scene Investigation unit. We hope that you and your students have enjoyed this interdisciplinary team investigation. We believe that as you and your students have worked throughout this project, you have seen the advantages and benefits of an interdisciplinary activity for your team teachers and students.

We have attempted to guide you through the Crime Scene Investigation step-by-step from the preparation activities to the courtroom trial. We also hope that as you and your fellow team teachers have been working your way through the activity, you have experienced the process and steps of putting together an interdisciplinary team activity. We hope that you may also use the unit as a model of how to develop and to organize your own interdisciplinary team activities.

Now that you have worked through the Crime Scene Investigation, you may be thinking of making some changes and adaptations or of creating your own investigation. In creating your own investigation, you can target specific goals and achievements for your team and students. In developing your own unit, you may want to consider the following:

- Using a location other than the library.
- Using several locations as crime scenes.
- Having an environmental crime.
- Bringing in different community resources.
- Having the crime consist of a stolen art exhibit.
- Using art experts to testify on the artwork.
- Involving the use of technology in the crime.

Enjoy trying your own crime scene!

Chapter Nineteen

Conclusion

We hope that the Crime Scene Investigation has been a rewarding experience for you and your students. There are many ways you can change and adapt this unit to meet the needs of your school and students.

We also hope that the Crime Scene Investigation has helped your students learn more about the Constitution and science techniques, and that it has stimulated interest in reading and writing. Perhaps your class now has many future lawyers, police officers, scientists, and news reporters. There may even be a best-selling mystery writer out there!

INDEX

About the Authors

Barbara Harris has been teaching English at Woodrow Wilson Middle School in Glendale, California, since 1971. She graduated from California State University, Northridge with a major in English and a minor in history. Five years ago, she joined Kris Kohlmeier and Bob Kiel to form an interdisciplinary team. They developed the Crime Scene Investigation Project, which has found enormous success as a teaching tool. In addition to being a favorite of their students, the Crime Scene Investigation Project won a 1996 Teaching Team–Grand Prize for Interdisciplinary Unit awarded by Prentice Hall and the National Middle School Association. The team has also lectured on the project before the California National League of Middle Schools. Barbara lives in Northridge, California, with her husband and two children.

Robert Kiel and his wife have lived in the Southern California area for most of their lives. They have been married for 27 years and have focused much of their time and energy in raising their three children. Robert's teaching career has blossomed in the time he has spent working with Barbara and Kris. "With team and school support, we have had the opportunity to maximize our efforts and provide the best educational program to our students," he says. "Their friendship has helped to make my profession a wonderful experience."

Kris Kohlmeier grew up in Glendale, California, in a family of teachers. He graduated from California State University, Northridge in 1985, earned his teaching credential in 1987, and began teaching at Woodrow Wilson Middle School, where he serves on many school district and leadership committees. He has taught physical education and social science since 1987. Kris has won various Teacher of the Year awards at Wilson. In 1996, he was appointed Mentor Teacher for the Glendale School District, and he was recognized with the Masonic Lodge Teacher Recognition Award in 1994.

from *Teacher Ideas Press*

CELEBRATING THE EARTH: Stories, Experiences, Activities
Norma J. Livo

Invite young readers to observe, explore, and appreciate the natural world through engaging activities. Livo shows you how to use folk stories, personal narrative, and a variety of learning projects to teach students about amphibians, reptiles, mammals, constellations, plants, and other natural phenomena. Designed to build a Naturalist Intelligence in young learners, these stories and activities are packed with scientific information. **All Levels.**
xvii, 174p. 8½x11 paper ISBN 1-56308-776-6

FAMOUS PROBLEMS AND THEIR MATHEMATICIANS
Art Johnson

Why did ordering an omelet cost one mathematician his life? The answer to this and other questions are found in this exciting new resource that shows your students how 60 mathematicians discovered mathematical solutions through everyday situations. These lessons are easily incorporated into the curriculum as an introduction to a math concept, a homework piece, or an extra challenge. Teacher notes and suggestions for the classroom are followed by extension problems and additional background material. **Grades 5–12.**
xvi, 179p. 8½x11 paper ISBN 1-56308-446-5

SCIENCE AND MATH BOOKMARK BOOK: 300 Fascinating, Fact-Filled Bookmarks
Kendall Haven and Roni Berg

Use these 300 reproducible bookmarks of fascinating facts, concepts, trivia, inventions, and discoveries to spark student learning. They cover all major disciplines of math and physical, earth, and life sciences—ready to copy, cut out, and give to your students. **Grades 4 and up.**
xii, 115p. 8½x11 paper ISBN 1-56308-675-1

WRITE RIGHT! Creative Writing Using Storytelling Techniques
Kendall Haven

Haven's breakthrough approach to creative writing uses storytelling techniques to enhance the creative writing process. This practical guide offers you directions for 38 writing exercises that will show students how to create powerful and dynamic fiction. All the steps are included, from finding inspiration and creating believable characters to the final edit. Activities are coded by levels, but most can be adapted to various grades. **All Levels.**
Xv, 213p. 8½x11 paper ISBN 1-56308-677-8

VISUAL MESSAGES: Integrating Imagery into Instruction
2d Edition
David M. Considine and Gail E. Haley

The authors provide effective media literacy strategies, activities, and resources that help students learn the critical-viewing skills necessary in our media-dominated world. Various media and types of programs are addressed, including motion pictures, television news, and advertising. Activities are coded by grade level and curriculum area. **Grades K–12.**
xxiii, 371p. 8½x11 paper ISBN 1-56308-575-5

For a free catalog or to place an order, please contact:
Teacher Ideas Press
Dept. B051 • P.O. Box 6633 • Englewood, CO • 80155-6633
800-237-6124 • www.lu.com/tip • Fax: 303-220-8843